# RORY GALLAGHER

# RORY
# GALLAGHER

*Jean-Noël Coghe*

MERCIER PRESS

Trade enquiries to COLUMBA MERCIER DISTRIBUTION,
55a Spruce Avenue, Stillorgan Industrial Park, Blackrock, Dublin

© EMP and Le Castor Astral
*English translation Lorna Carson and Brian Steer*

ISBN: 1 85635 387 7

10 9 8 7 6

TO SYLVIE-ANNE (ON TOUR WITH HIM)
THANKS TO MARTINE FOR HER SUPPORT, HER PATIENCE
TO LESLIE FOR NATHACHA'S SMILE
TO JENNIFER FOR HER EFFICIENT HELP.
TO OTHERS FOR THEIR PRESENCE, THEIR ABSENCE . . .

*Printed in Ireland by Colour Books Ltd.*

# Contents

# Anonymous Preface

To Mimile, One Evening with the Blues ...

The vast, dark interior of the disused, soulless hangar smelt stuffy. A slight odour of beer mixed with a more powerful one of dope. The place was packed though, that night.

It wasn't easy pushing through this strange but unthreatening crowd: a ragged collection of young men and women, who glanced at me without really looking, maybe a little surprised to see me there that night, but understanding that I, despite appearances, also had every right to love it.

A kind of tacit understanding hung over the waiting throng, all perfectly conscious of what they had come there to hear: a rare species of unworldly Irish poet, musician first and foremost, seeking only to be rewarded with the same warmth that he spread around him, who unblushingly poured his heart out with his guitar.

I was no musician myself, of course. I knew nothing about technique, but somehow or other it was so comforting to feel the pleasure in playing which he put over, that no more was needed in order to love him.

So chord followed chord, sometimes too fast for my liking, sometimes too loud for my tastes, but, transported by the music, I felt good. And then suddenly, without warning, the poet would be laid bare, and alone with nothing except his battered old guitar, or his golden-brown mandolin, his bottleneck slide in his hand, the troubadour would blow like the wind through his harmonica, and would sing us a melody so sad it made us cry.

At first, it could almost have been a joke, but no, Gallagher had opened himself up heart and soul, and I could almost have cried. It went on for ages and yet the crowd still shouted for more ...

I was just twenty-five, and I had all this poetry singing round my head. It seemed like it could never end ...

But still, he died.

I can cry now, Rory ... I can cry.

Éric

*I have never met the author of these lines. When Rory passed away, I received a number of letters, telephone calls, drawings and photos, including this text. It says it all; there is nothing to add. Each time I read it, I'm overwhelmed. I still cry, to this day.*

*Rory receives his first wooden guitar*

# THE KID

Regal, frozen in midflight, he hung motionless – his immense wings spread wide and majestic – hanging noiselessly in the air. Far down beneath him, a flock of screeching seagulls followed a small fishing boat that left foam-white furrows in its wake. Moving unhurriedly but noisily up the channel to the throbbing, spluttering rhythm of its engine, the boat gave off clouds of blue-tinted exhaust fumes and an acrid smell of diesel.

Rory strode up the main street and over one of the many stone bridges that criss-cross the River Lee, whose journey ends in the sea here, at Cork. Once on the quay, Rory continued along past the row of houses that faced the canal.

Still hanging in the sky above, the seagull let out a cry before swooping down over Rory. It beat its outstretched wings, raising its head, and soared away out of sight, engulfed by a cloud.

Rory was unsettled – happy and nervous at the same time – for he had met the object of his desires, the stuff of his dreams. He had met her but was she within his reach? Would fate bring them together? Since he'd noticed her, she had never left his thoughts. At that very instant she had seduced him, put a spell on him. Time after time, he had come alone to the quayside to spy on her, to admire and adore her. He could stand it no longer; he had to decide for once and for all to do something about it, to make her his own. But what would his mother, Mona, say? What could he say to convince such an upright, ladylike woman who had put up with so much already?

Ireland without its music would not be Ireland; there has always been music in Ireland and Rory had been steeped in music since his birth. He was born on 2 March 1948 in Ballyshannon, County Donegal, ironically at the Rock Hospital, where a commemorative plaque was unveiled to mark the fact after a ceremony in June 2000. He was also christened at the Rock Church. Rory's father, Daniel, was himself a musician; it was in his blood. Daniel passed his passion for music to Rory and breathed into him the energy necessary to feed that passion. Rory's parents gave him his first real wooden guitar when they moved to Cork, the birthplace of his mother, when he was eight years old. It was an unusual choice of instrument for such a young boy, but his mother had not disapproved. Rory showed himself to be a gifted and devoted musician – and never to the detriment of his schoolwork. He appreciated the ballads that his mother liked, and had great respect for the traditional music that had been the background to her youth and gave order to her life during a troubled, unsettled time not long ago. It was a music that sang of hope but was redolent of fear, sadness, pain and death – Irish blues.

But her son's tastes took him increasingly towards a style of music that surprised and disquieted her; a swaying, breathless music played by black or white Americans in a flood of rhythmic guitars.

Rory began to master the guitar from the age of nine. First he learnt how to handle the six strings. He worked his way through them patiently, for hours at a time. He would place his fingers on the neck of the guitar and run them up and down, honing his dexterity, plucking the steel wires, racing through chords, sharpening the tone. Rory practised ceaselessly, refining his playing and his speed. Lonnie Donegan was his idol. His greatest heroes were skiffle players – skiffle was a cross between folk music and country music. Soon Rory appeared in public, at school concerts, in nursing homes, at family occasions in his parish and other such venues.

At twelve years old Rory was already open to all kinds of music. Through listening to their records, he discovered Elvis Presley, Eddie Cochran, Buddy Holly, Gene Vincent and Chuck Berry amongst others. Rock and roll was a blend of folk music brought to the States by settlers – notably the Irish – and of music emanating from the slave population. It was a form of musical expression that suited Rory perfectly, there was no denying it, although it also brought him his share of disappointments. At this early age, his repertoire included standards by people like Roy Rodgers, Lonnie Donegan and Chuck Berry, but also more controversial numbers and there were people who scarcely approved of a boy of his age plucking his guitar to lyrics that were hardly appropriate: lyrics packed with overtly sexual connotations. His interpretation of *Living Doll* by Cliff Richard and the Drifters was riddled with unsuitable phrases.

Rory asked his younger brother, Donal, to play and sing harmony with him. They formed a duo and a skiffle group with other pals and did some well-received songs like 'Wake Up Little Suzie' by the Everly Brothers. Donal, however, was not musician material and their collaboration didn't last. The two Gallagher brothers, who otherwise adored each other, ended up arguing on stage! So Rory formed a band with school friends, already wielding his guitar with a calloused hand.

Walking faster now, Rory greeted one or two people on his way, but avoided a group of girls for fear of being held up. Rory loved this small lively city on the Atlantic coast. Its population of over 150,000 inhabitants were mainly working-class, employed in the service industries, tourism, agriculture and Ford cars. There were as many distilleries as dairies, where whiskeys such as Paddy and Powers aged in oak casks. Murphy's and Beamish stout were also brewed in the city. The surrounding countryside of green, rolling hills and valleys was dotted with austere monuments reflecting the influence of the Catholic Church. Cork was a town of contrasts. It had always been known as the Rebel County, with strong Republican support, and was famous for its very particular sense of humour. The fine, penetrating grey drizzle made the cobblestones shine, and the bright sunlight bathed the winding streets, warming the stones, invading the surrounding countryside and marking out unique contours. Light and shade. The toughness and tenderness.

Nothing would deflect Rory from his path. He did not have the time to linger in front of the posters at the cinema displaying the image of one of his favourites, James Dean. 'Great,' he thought to himself, 'they're showing *East of Eden*'. Since his childhood he had regularly gone into the dark interior, more often than not to see musicals. 'I saw a lot of guitarists in those films,' he said, 'and thought that it was the ideal instrument to express the music I liked to listen to. It could be because I wanted to sing that I turned to the guitar. It was the best instrument for that. It is difficult to sing while playing the drums, for instance.' He went into his grandparents' pub and climbed the stairs to the flat where his parents lived, to find his brother Donal and tell him his secret, persuading him to help. Donal agreed to accompany Rory and they both set off in the direction of the quays.

Rory walked faster and faster until he caught sight of the shop sign. His quest for the Holy Grail was almost over. 'I hope she's still there!' At the shop front, he stopped and looked in the window, holding his breath. His eyes swept from left to right, right to left. Where was she? There! She was still waiting for him.

The brothers went in as Rory looked admiringly in her direction. She stood proudly in front of the shop window, looking so sure of herself. Rory, on the other hand, was trembling with emotion as he held out his hand to touch her. She was unique and meant only for him. Rory had never dreamt that he would find her right there in Cork. In fact, she had ended up there almost by accident (or more likely by heavenly design!) ordered by another musician on tour with his showband. Having had the precise model that he wanted shipped especially over from the United States, the client had come back and decided that he didn't like the brown colour and had insisted on re-ordering a red one like that used by Hank Marvin of the Shadows. He had taken the original guitar to play for two months while he was waiting for the other one, and had then brought it back and exchanged it. Since then the Stratocaster had remained in the shop, rejected. To the consternation of the owner, Michael Crowley, it was placed in the shop window as a second hand instrument.

Michael slid up behind Rory. He knew the Gallagher brothers as being part of a trustworthy and well-respected family, and he was a businessman. Rory told him that he was interested in buying the guitar but it cost £100, a small fortune for anyone. Without flinching, he proposed a part-exchange deal with his own Rosatti guitar as down payment and the rest in instalments.

He had recently joined a band called the Fontana, made up of six musicians, some of whom were semi-professionals. There were plenty of concerts to be played and even if the fees were as yet rather modest, Rory made some money. He agreed to hand it over to pay off the hire-purchase. Michael Crowley accepted the deal.

Invited by Michael to try out the guitar, Rory hesitated before lifting it off its stand. Surprised by how light it was, he held it in position against him and ran his fingers over the neck, teasing the strings. His head bent in concentration, everything around him faded into the background until he was alone with his guitar, Rory the kid and his mythical Fender Stratocaster 61. He could almost feel the pounding of his heart echo in the wooden body of the guitar, sure that everyone around, Michael, the owner, his own brother, Donal, even the other clients in the store, must be able to hear it too. Overwhelmed with joy he held his now most treasured, most trusty possession close to his chest. It was 1963. Rory was fifteen years old. The guitar would be with him until his death.

# MINING COUNTRY

The south-east of Ireland was not as strongly affected by the industrial revolution as the north of France. The relative lack of change witnessed there contrasts sharply with the devastating upheaval that took place in the Nord-Pas-de-Calais region of France. There the terraced houses of the mining villages used to wake up, according to the season, to the spitting, cold rain or the singing birds of early dawn. Soon, the military-style rows of dirty brick houses stretching from the church to the mine-head would light up and shortly afterwards pour their contingents of men out onto the pavement to trudge in procession up the road to take possession of the bowels of the earth, the younger ones in anxious trepidation, the older ones (although 'old' is a relative term, between the damp and silicosis), resigned.

The women, married or single, mothers or childless, would also be setting off, towards the main square where buses, their engines purring amid the smell of rancid diesel fumes, would be waiting in the dawn gloom to take them off to Roubaix, Tourcoing or Wattrelos. A fifty-kilometre round trip every day to plunge them into the deafening noise of the weaving industry, into the towering monuments to textile, whose proud red-brick chimneys – like spires of an industrialisation gone mad – dominated the surrounding terraced houses which teemed with more workers who were just as badly off. Blinded by arrogance, the industry, though still flourishing, persisted in ignoring its own impending distress, for very soon these two centres of exploitation were to crush and cast aside their respective workforces. The economic crisis was looming large on the horizon but nobody seemed to care, although those doing the exploiting were nevertheless taking the care to re-invest their capital elsewhere, while the exploited slaved away, worked themselves into the ground and ruined their health, as yet unaware of the fate that awaited them, suffering with dignity as they dreamed of better days to come.

At the weekends, dressed up-to-the-nines, they were transformed. The Sunday morning market would be packed with people. If a ray of sunlight managed to pierce through the clouds it would bring with it an almost festive atmosphere, and the strains of an accordion could even be heard coming from the music stall. As the church bells rang out men could be seen selling the communist party newsletter. Women went to pray, but eventually everyone met up in the local bistro for a pre-lunch tipple. The betting shops would fill up as, with beaming smiles, glasses were emptied down necks tightly cramped into starched shirt collars and ties.

As they enjoyed yet another beer or pastis, tickets were brandished. 'This time, this'll be the one,' they would all be thinking. Some would bet to win, while others would content themselves with an each-way flutter. Hope springs eternal. Shouts and laughter would fill the air with noisy conversation, northern intonations replying to Italian, Polish and North African accents, for such were the successive immigrants brought in to do the dirty work and to insure the wealth of a 'Madame France' who was not always grateful.

At fourteen, whether they had passed or failed the school certificate, all boys were allowed one cigarette before being thrown into the clutches of the 'Man-eater' and down into the pit. First, they went through the Hang Man's room, where they would be kitted out with overalls, and then they would queue up at the counter to get a number etched onto a tiny tin dog tag which was to be worn at all times to enable identification in case of an accident. Next, they would walk single file towards the liftshaft, their stomachs knotted with fear, pushed from behind until a metal grill slammed shut, a hooter sounded and the cage dropped them down into the depths of the earth amid a hellish din. The helmeted men armed with pick axes stood packed together in stern silence and a sickening heat as the darkness swallowed them up until only the dim, flickering light from their lamps remained to illuminate their sullen, nervous faces. One last shudder, a squeal of brakes, and the grill opened to let the men disappear off into the dark tunnels. 'Oh, look, a mouse … that's a good sign, that means there's no gas!'

Meanwhile the girls would be rattling through the night in their armada of buses wedged onto leatherette seats. Some would be trying to pour themselves a steaming cup of coffee from a thermos flask while others nodded off quietly or daydreamed. They had been landed with the nickname of 'miners' daughters', which carried with it the obvious connotation of 'loose women', an insult that did not detract from their spirit. Amid the damp heat and throbbing hum of the machines they were often targets of the taunts, jibes and lewd suggestions of their male colleagues. Some of the girls had quite attractive shapely figures, just visible under their nylon overalls, and they would often be on the receiving end of looks, smiles and wandering hands, but they tended to save their energy for the excesses of the weekend that lay ahead.

As soon as Friday came around, the youngsters would be out on the town, the beer flowing in ramshackle night-clubs improvised in the back rooms of pubs, cafés or former cinemas. In this particular moth-eaten hall it was Patricia Carli who could be heard giving her all, singing '*Arrête, arrête, ne me touche pas, je t'en supplie, aie pitié de moi!*' ('Stop, stop, don't touch me, I beg of you, take pity on me!') as couples kissed and cuddled amidst the smell of sweat, tobacco, drink and cheap perfume, the walls running with damp, the nauseating stench of the urinals filling the air every time the back door opened. Leaning against the bar of this over-packed hall was Noeghan Jelcoe, not yet seventeen years old, listening, wide-eyed, to a conversation between the owner of the joint and the rather fat man in the blue suit with a cigar hanging from the corner of his mouth who had dragged him there in the first place. Noeghan felt completely out of his depth, in another universe, far removed from his home in Wattrelos where the girls from the Catholic school École des Sœurs went about in pleated skirts and bobby socks. Here the girls were parading around in mini-skirts and fishnet tights with backcombed hair and heavy eye make-up, going to the toilets in giggling gangs, pushing past the watching boys ready to fight over them at the drop of a hat. Noeghan couldn't take his eyes off these girls, trying to stare surreptitiously at them like he would in the evenings at the factory gates where he and his mates went sometimes on their mopeds to lie in wait for them, fishing for a glance, a smile or a sign from the girls before they climbed onto the bus. Sometimes a girl would wave back, making fun of them in a hail of cackles, or even fix a date to which they never turned up, and all this amidst the incredible chaos of the night shift taking over from the afternoon shift; thousands of people passing each other going in opposite directions, weaving between mobile street stalls and shops that stayed open until nightfall, getting in and out of dozens of buses, beating out the rhythm of the neighbourhood.

Flicking cigar ash on the floor of the bar Jean Vanloo tried to persuade the man opposite that as far he was concerned it was groups that held the key to the future, that they were in demand from young people and that more halls, like the one he was in, should adapt to accommodate them. Vanloo knew what he was talking about. He not only managed the Belgian dancehall that was the most popular with youngsters from the French border towns of Roubaix-Tourcoing, but also the group the Sunlights, as well as having just produced the recent tour of France and Belgium by Gene Vincent, Noeghan's hero. Every evening after school he would slip off to where the Sunlights lived and go to their rehearsals, discovering records by Eddie

*The Fontana, Rory's first group*

Cochran and Buddy Holly, even getting to meet Vince Taylor and strum on Moustique's exact copy of Cochran's Gretch guitar.

Vanloo finally got what he was after and managed to persuade club-owners to let groups appear there. The variety shows their fathers had watched were coming to an end. The stages were being taken over by groups in lame suits with their drums and guitars doing six-hour-long, uninterrupted concerts to which the young people came in droves. Dancehalls were mushrooming along with groups, of which the Sunlights were the best-loved. Noeghan followed them everywhere and wrote about them in the regional paper. Little by little he no longer contented himself with just looking at the 'miners' daughters' that he met.

## RORY

Donal looked on admiringly, with bated breath, as Rory slowly lifted up the lid of the long, flat case that contained his treasure. Her shining metal and varnished wood appeared, lying on a red velvet bed. Rory seized the guitar and held her up like a banner confirming that she was at least his own, his sword of light!

Michael Crowley had, however, given Rory a document – to be signed by his mother as a formal guarantee and to be returned to him – confirming the terms of the agreement. Rory and Donal had agreed without hesitation, before leaving while the going was good, knowing full well that it would be difficult to persuade their mother to give such an authorisation. Thus, a forged signature offered by an anonymous hand was more than welcome. The two brothers were once again accomplices with perfectly clear consciences, since Rory genuinely felt he needed the guitar. It was something he could not explain that was etched into his very being, and Donal trusted him implicitly, never doubting him for an instant, feeling instinctively, somehow, the symbolic solemnity of the moment.

Rory grabbed the lead and plugged one jack into the guitar and the other into the old, patched-up Selmer Truvoice twelve-watt amplifier, which let out a screeching *'Craaaash!'*, followed by a piercing whistle. It was a makeshift amp that Rory had pulled apart, messed around with, transformed and modified in order to get the maximum power and vigour out of the Fender. With a deafening crash, the first notes and chords crackled together, the guitar was given its baptism of fire, and Rory and Donal embarked on a clandestine life, for it was imperative that they hide the existence of the guitar from their mother. Whenever Rory got the chance after school, he would run up to their bedroom, take it out from its hiding place under the bed and wonder at it, taking in the smell of polish that permeated the atmosphere, admiring the venerated instrument lying on its bed of red velvet like some sort of religious relic. Moments such as those would take on an almost mystical quality. But mothers will be mothers, and Mona Gallagher inevitably discovered the object and angrily demanded an explanation. Rory set about convincing her that he was determined to become a musician, a guitarist, and not only a back-line, rhythm guitarist content to accompany others, but a soloist, living and breathing his own music. For Rory, the guitar embodied his very destiny: he'd had no choice but to buy it. Donal spoke up for his brother, trying to talk his mother round until finally she relented and allowed Rory to keep the guitar, on two conditions: firstly, that he keep his word and pay back Michael Crowley, and secondly, that he stop playing during the opening hours of his grandparents' pub and scaring the regulars.

The press were singing the praises of the Fontana Showband, with a four-column photo in the local Cork paper, the six of them smiling in their suits and ties and short, neatly brushed hair. The accompanying article described a group of musicians, including a brass section, who could be seen playing all the old favourites, contemporary hits and even rock-and-roll numbers in numerous dances and concerts in and around the region. The members of the band had all

**FONTANA SHOWBAND, CORK**

Photo by Jacques, Cork,

*(Above) The Fontana, under Rory's influence, changes its image, and (below) changes the name of the group on its posters. The Fontana becomes The Impact*

*The* INNISFAIL
IRISH SOCIAL CLUB
700 HIGH ROAD, LEYTONSTONE, E.11
(Between The Red Lion and The Green Man)
2 mins. Leytonstone Underground

GRAND
**Bank-Holiday Programme**

**Sunday, 29th August**

# THE IMPACT
## SHOWBAND
FORMERLY
### THE FABULOUS
# FONTANA
## SHOWBAND
**From CORK**

Dancing Saturday, Sunday, Monday

turned professional, with the exception of the young guitarist Rory Gallagher, who was still at school. Rory was the only one who refused to wear the band's uniform.

Being a pupil in a religious school, Rory had lessons all morning but was free to rehearse most afternoons. The Fontana worked hard on their repertoire, trying to recreate, note for note, the cover versions of popular songs they played. It was tedious work, but enabled them to play in public for hours on end. Although this was good practice for Rory, it did not leave much room for improvisation. Helped by such a professional-looking guitar, Rory's reputation was growing, and he was increasingly in demand, learning about group dynamics, different types of audiences and their demands, and various styles of music, while at the same time meeting a lot of other musicians.

Not all was rosy, however, and it was far from a risk-free apprenticeship. One night, in an out-of-the-way village, the Fontana walked straight into a storm. The artist supposed to be topping the bill failed to turn up, and a mixture of alcohol and plain stupidity had whipped the crowd into such frenzy that they started to boo off the support band that was already on stage. The Fontana were thus on the receiving end of jeers and insults, as well as bottles and any other projectiles that the increasingly hostile crowd could lay their hands on, until the crowd got completely out of control and started getting up on stage to take it out on the musicians and their instruments. Seeing this, Rory threw himself on his beloved Stratocaster, choosing to take the punches and kicks that rained down upon him in order to protect his most precious possession, rather than see it destroyed. The guitar was thus saved, but Rory came out of the incident badly hurt. As a result, he fell ill and was obliged to take two weeks off school, which, in turn, meant that the Christian Brothers had to be given a reason for his absence. On learning the truth, they were furious that a pupil of theirs should be seen in public with musicians playing rock-and-roll – the devil's music that preyed on the youth of Ireland. For them, he had gone too far, and they decided to make him an example to the others.

So when he finally returned to school, the Brothers took out all their hatred and impotence on Rory in an effort to *correct* him, by means of beatings with a blackthorn stick. Once more, he took the punishment without saying a word, bottling everything up inside him. It was not until a few days later, when Donal noticed the cuts on his brother's legs, that anyone found out what had happened. When asked about it, Rory simply replied that it really didn't matter. But it did, because one of his legs became badly infected, swelling up like a balloon, until Donal got so worried that he had no choice but to tell his mother about it. Rory was therefore obliged to describe to his mother the punishment he had been given. She was furious, and decided to withdraw him from the school, placing him in a private school, St Kieran's College, which had a blind headmaster, Mr Leahy, who later became lord mayor of Cork. The school wasn't run by a religious order and the rules of the game were made clear from the outset: Rory was one day to become a professional musician and was therefore to be allowed time off to follow the group whenever necessary. Any instances of Rory being late were to be accepted without question, and the teachers were to give their word that he would be punished for neither. For his part, Rory promised to do at least enough schoolwork to keep up with the rest of his classmates, and he passed his exams with honours.

## MERSEYSIDE

At around the same time, in a harbour town on the opposite side of the Irish Sea, a group called the Beatles were making waves with what was becoming known as the Mersey Beat – a lively, colourful, rhythmic music influenced by Buddy Holly, Gene Vincent, Eddie Cochran, Little Richard, *et al.* The established English rockers like Tommy Steele, Lonnie Donegan, Billy Fury, Cliff Richard, Marty Wilde, Adam Faith and Joe Brown, who had hitherto contented themselves with imitating the American masters, were being swept away by the new tide of Liverpudlian bands. Not only did they adapt the existing rock classics to their own peculiar style of music, they also rapidly produced their own, original-sounding compositions.

The music business was turned on its head and the young people quickly took this new music on board. Liverpool's famous Cavern Club, a small, red-brick cellar in a cul-de-sac in the centre of town where it was all said to have started, was never empty, and similar venues were quickly establishing themselves. The professionals of the record industry were losing touch, and the new groups were dragging fresh, young, ambitious producers and managers along with them in their wake, including names such as Epstein, Oldham and Gomelski. It would only take a short time, however, for the large companies to wake up to what was happening and start clawing their way back, opening their studio doors to these long-haired hordes. The streets were suddenly paved with recording contracts bringing together acts like the Dave Clark Five, Gerry and the Pacemakers, Herman's Hermits, the Hollies and Manfred Mann under the reins of one recording studio or another. Also, around this time, pirate radio stations such as Radio Caroline, Radio London and Radio Scotland started reinventing radio broadcasting and bombarding the airwaves with the new sounds. The DJs were kings of these new sounds, and the BBC was almost strangled to death before slowly managing to readapt.

London too was ringing the changes: around Soho, jazz clubs, such as the 100 Club and Flamingo, had to co-exist with the Marquee Club, where bands including the Rolling Stones and the Yardbirds overthrew all preconceived ideas about pop music. Tracks were no longer the standard two minutes long but were starting to last up to four and a half, even six minutes. And it was no passing fad or flash in the pan, it was a veritable revolution – a phenomenon that was growing louder daily: in Newcastle the Animals had raised their heads and roared, while in Birmingham the Moody Blues had appeared.

From the districts and suburbs of London sprang the self-sufficient Kinks, the self-adoring Pretty Faces, the self-inflicting Who and the self-important Small Faces, who, each in their own way, served to establish the concept of the Mods – a generation of trendy young things dressed in the latest fashions. Sporting tight-fitting, drainpipe trousers, moccasins and fishtail parkas, they cruised around Carnaby Street during the week on their motorbikes popping little blue pills, while at the weekends they would go down to the beach at Brighton on the south coast for a 'rumble', clashing with gangs of Rockers in leather jackets riding scooters. Mary Quant was dressing the street kids, Twiggy was knocking 'em dead on the catwalks, and the group If had just given Lindsay Anderson the perfect vehicle to reveal Malcolm McDowell. Perfidious Albion was losing her way and gradually going mad.

Each new group brought with it its own particular style of music, but all of them were inspired by the black music of artists like Chuck Berry and Bo Diddley: music with a swing in its beat, accompanied by maracas and sometimes a harmonica. The rhythm and blues of Bobby Bland, James Brown and Otis Redding was also a great influence. Bands started focusing on the Hammond organ and brass sections, leading to artists such as Zoot Money or Georgie Fame flirting with types of jazz. Some went even further back into the roots of music, plunging themselves into the blues. John Lee Hooker, Muddy Waters and Robert Johnson were highly regarded, and John Mayall and his Bluesbreakers were beginning their crusade.

Belfast had not been left out of the picture. The band Them launched Van Morrison. Things were swinging in Cork, too. The Fontana repertoire stretched from Jim Reeves covers to adaptations of Georgie Fame numbers. Rory was more inclined towards tracks like Chuck Berry's 'Nadine' or 'Brown-Eyed Handsome Man', and his influence over the group was increasing. A noticeable change was taking place. The band members were all dressed in black suits, with long hair, their faces on stage set in serious concentration. The rhythm-and-blues influence was undeniable. To complete the metamorphosis,

First of the NEW WAVE—

IMPACT
*Showband* CORK

Manager— J. Philip Prendergast Phone Cork 20140

*The metamorphosis is complete. The Impact evolves musically, changes era*

SATURDAY                    21st AUGUST

*Two Band Session*

## THE
## IMPACT
## SHOWBAND
(CORK)

*Supported by*

## THE TROPICAL SHOWBAND

★     FREE COACH SERVICE     ★
Special coaches leaving from ballroom at half hour intervals
from 1 a.m. to 3 a.m. SUNDAY LATE DANCES and on
★  EVERY SATURDAY to facilitate patrons to Kilburn, Cricklewood,  ★
Willesden, Hammersmith, Acton and Ealing.

the group changed its name to the Impact, and they were regularly called upon to play support for passing groups like the Everly Brothers, the Animals, the Byrds and many more.

As the number of concerts increased, Rory had less and less time for school, and in 1965 the band went abroad for the first time, to Spain. They had a contract to play at an American airbase near Madrid. It was a heady experience for Rory, as it was the first chance he'd had to measure himself against an American audience. He passed the test with flying colours. In a letter to Donal back in Ireland, however, he did mention his frustration over one dark cloud that cast a shadow over the evening: the Beatles had been playing in concert in Madrid that same night and he'd been unable to go!

Back in Cork, the Impact had another problem. It was Lent. All the clubs were temporarily shut, at the instigation of the clergy, which meant that, as the churches all filled, the pockets of the musicians and the dance-hall owners, emptied.

To get through this period of fasting, the musicians and sinners were left with only one alternative – to get on the boat bound for England, to leave for the next six weeks. Rory came up with another idea: to use the north London clubs as merely a stepping stone en route to Hamburg and the mythical Star Club, following in the footsteps of the Beatles. Once in London, however, things did not go according to plan. Only one or two small, badly paid concerts were on offer, and the musicians, tired, hungry and broke, were at the end of their tether. Arguments broke out in the group and the brass section decided to quit. Rory, backed only by the bassist and the drummer, was faced with the choice of returning to Ireland, staying in London or carrying on to Germany. A lightweight contract to do one or two dates in some obscure German clubs tipped the balance, and the pilgrimage continued. When the band turned up minus three of their musicians, the promoter was understandably a little worried, but Rory managed to quell his suspicions by telling him that the others had gone down with a bad case of the flu, and the first concert went ahead. The trio was a roaring success and the promoter was delighted, giving them an extended series of concerts around the country.

# DOURGES

The athletically built, short-haired primary-school teacher, dressed in neat corduroys and a casual jacket, crossed the playground. His eyes betrayed the tiredness of a hard night's decision-making. As she put their little daughter to bed, his wife, Simone, a firm-handed woman who worked for the Inland Revenue, had told him to consider his responsibilities, but reluctantly promised her support in whatever he decided. His friend, neighbour and confidant, Mario, had actively encouraged him to do it, as had Boro, a sometimes unruly ex-pupil who had knocked around the clubs playing a bit of guitar. And so finally he had decided: he was going to go for it. Albert Warin paused, took a deep breath and smiled. 'Let's do it,' he whispered to himself, before disappearing into the classroom as if nothing had happened.

Dourges is a mining community in the Pas de Calais region of France, situated about thirty kilometres from Lille. The town is wedged between towering slag heaps, which today are green and overgrown, and the main Lille-to-Paris motorway. At the end of the 1960s, the mining industry was already in decline, although coal extraction still continued. The north of France, located as it was on the geographical front line just the other side of the Channel, was being badly affected by the British boom. Along with neighbouring Belgium and

Paris, it did benefit from certain offshoots of the revolution. The region was being swamped by pirate radio station broadcasts and found itself part of the music scene's avant-garde. Dancehalls were being transformed into nightclubs, following in the footsteps of Jean Vanloo and his Mouscron haunt, who had turned his Relais de la Poste into the Twenty Club, which quickly rose to be on a par with the Marquee or the Star Club, attracting DJs from Radio Caroline as well as many well-respected groups.

Vanloo had taken Noeghan Jelcoe along on the Sunlights' journey to London, where, in February 1965, they became the first French group to record there. At the Marquee Club, they discovered and met a group called the Yardbirds, and Vanloo immediately set about organising mini concert tours for them and the Animals, the Kinks, the Moody Blues, the Zombies, the Small Faces and Jimi Hendrix, amongst others. Groups quickly made a habit of slipping unofficially back and forth across the Franco-Belgian border to play in clubs such as the Eden Ranch in France's mining area. Noeghan Jelcoe often went along to gather material for the articles he wrote in the music magazine *Disco Revue*, the first of its kind to be published in French. As time went by, musical tastes were steadily changing, and the young people who filled the clubs to dance, drink, flirt and let their hair down were starting to call for a more passionate, rhythmic music than was being served up to them. Fashions were changing, and rhythm and blues, with its impressive brass sections, was increasingly in demand.

It was at this time, in Dourges, that Albert Warin had just decided to bring the musical education of the young people of the community up to date by breaking into his savings, buying an old run-down cinema, rolling up his sleeves and, with a little help from his friends, launching himself into a new adventure. At the end of 1967, a few months of digging, rebuilding and painting later, Albert the schoolteacher opened the Ram Dam Club.

# TASTE

Rory had come to a decision. His apprenticeship with the Fontana Showband, and then the Impact, had run its course, and he was starting to feel the need to break away on his own and shoulder responsibility for the music he felt within him. A simple lead guitar, bass and drum trio seemed to him the ideal format to express the music that he felt beating in his heart. Thus, Rory formed the band Taste.

The two young Cork musicians with whom he took up the challenge had music in their blood as much as he did. Norman Damery on drums, and Eric Kitteringham on bass guitar, had been members of the same highly rated Cork-based group, the Axels, and their views on music and also the manner in which to pursue it were similar to Rory's. They considered Cork too limited in its possibilities and agreed that it was time to venture further afield.

*Rory's first appearance in a trio, with Taste*

They opted for the strategy used by Liverpool groups like the Beatles and decided to go on the road, to preach their word in any club that was willing to listen, however measly the fee and however

*Taste; from left to right: Norman, Rory, Eric*

bad the conditions. So, they packed their very basic equipment into the back of an old banger – very often with a friend at the wheel, because Rory couldn't drive – and set off across the country. Hard though it proved to be, the satisfaction that they felt at the various crowds' enthusiasm more than made up for it. They went relentlessly backwards and forwards to different clubs, playing a repertoire consisting of blues classics and Rory's own compositions, and soon built themselves a solid reputation. Avoiding Dublin, they chose to concentrate their efforts on the Belfast area, where they knew that Rory's music would be more readily appreciated. In Belfast itself, they managed to negotiate a residency at the Maritime Blues Club, founded by Van Morrison but now run by Eddie Kennedy, following Van's departure to London. On their opening night, the band went down a storm, and the young audience loved them. From then on, the club was packed to the rafters every night.

A figure stood watching as the lights came on and a shiver of anticipation went through the awaiting audience, who turned to face the now brightly lit amps and drum kit. The background music was turned off and the noise of the crowd slowly subsided. Three jean-clad characters with long hair took their places on stage, the drummer tested the tension of his skins, the bass started humming and the lead guitarist plugged in his Fender, producing a shrill whistle of feedback before advancing towards his microphone and greeting the audience. Then they let rip with the music.

The figure below them looked on intently, noticing with interest

*Taste – from left to right, Eric Kittringham (bass), Norman Damery (drums), Rory (guitar)*

28

# The Taste

## the local scene

## Taste For Success?

RECOGNISE the faces? Yes they're three popular guys on the Cork beat club scene. That's Rory Gallagher (Ex-Impact) in the centre and he's flanked by two ex-members of the Axills, Erik and Norman.

The three have got together to form a new group and they're calling themselves The Taste (well by now we're used to odd names, bad or good, in the group world).

As a trio they differ from most of their contemporaries which are usually four or five piece groups, and they promise that their music will be original too. Here's wishing them luck.

INTRODUCING CORK'S LATEST—
### THE TASTE
Imperial Hotel, Saturday, 8—12
Admission 5/-.    Rights of Admission Reserved.

The Best Yet ——
RORY
ERIC  **TASTE**  NORMAN
THE
PLUS MARTELLS
Dancing 8—12    TO-NIGHT (SAT.)    Adm. 5/-.
**IMPERIAL HOTEL**

FIRST booking as the TASTE.

*Page extract from notebook kept by Donal Gallagher, in which he has collected information concerning Taste*

the rapt attention of the watching public and their reactions to the sparkling solos. He soon realised he was witnessing something special. 'It's true what they're saying about these three,' he whispered under his breath.

The owner, a friend of his who had put him on to the group, spotted him and gave him a thumbs-up sign. He had to admit that the man had not been exaggerating: there certainly was an indefinable quality about the passion and vigour of the guitarist.

29

*Rory, Isle of Wight, 1970*

At the end of the set, he introduced himself to the musicians. Having listened intently to what the man had to say, the singer-guitarist conferred with the other band members and they agreed with the proposition. So it was that a few days later Rory and his band went to meet record producer Mervyn Solomon, as arranged, at his recording studio, having agreed to make some demo tapes.

They paid scant attention to the structuring of the numbers, simply laying them down one after another in no particular order; the professional takes would come later. The initial recordings finished, they were shipped off to Solomon's brother Phil, who was in charge of distribution for an Irish record label, Major Minor Records, a subsidiary of Decca Records. Without consulting Rory, a few tracks were put on the market. Rory was appalled by this.

The demo tape was eventually brought out as an album under the title *Taste, In The Beginning*. On the sleeve of the record released on the French market, the musicians are stated as being Norman Damery and Eric Kitteringham, whereas on the German version these names have disappeared, replaced by John Wilson and Richard McCracken, two future members of Taste! Rory was sickened and incensed by this but was powerless to do anything about it, having no say as to what could be done with the recording, which had, for him, been merely a rehearsal, a working recording, not a final take. There was just one thing that reassured Rory a little in this whole shoddy, incident: on the back of one of the sleeves was a blurb explaining that the remainder of the tracks originally recorded during the same session had inadvertently been destroyed!

## TASTE: TAKE 2

The group continued touring at home and overseas, wherever their mood, and chance meetings, took them, notably in Germany, which was at that time swarming with American military bases, clubs and discos. Conditions were not always easy and the band members sometimes went hungry, often sleeping in their mini-van. It was a gruelling lifestyle, 'but it was great', as Rory later confessed. Taste regularly got the chance to play alongside artists like Cream, Peter Green's Fleetwood Mac or John Mayall, and back on their home turf they were not to be missed. Eddie Kennedy of the Maritime Club [now renamed Club Rado] became their manager and got them numerous contracts in London, notably at the Marquee. One evening, an A&R man from Polydor Records was in the audience, and he was very taken with what he saw. After a recording studio audition he offered Rory an album deal on the spot, but with one condition: Rory was to replace the other two musicians in the trio with drummer John Wilson and bassist Richard McCracken. It was a non-negotiable, take-it-or-leave-it deal. Rory was devastated. He considered Norman and Eric to be more than capable of doing a good job on the recording. On the other hand, it was the opportunity of a lifetime to record the album he had so longed for. Besides, Wilson and McCracken had stage and recording experience: Wilson had drummed with Van Morrison's Them, for example. He and McCracken would provide a very strong base from which Rory could evolve much more quickly. After a lot of soul-searching, Rory decided that it was a chance he could not afford to throw away. He accepted, and a new chapter had begun. Taste 2 was formed.

## RORY THE KID

Donal shut the large, grey, hardback exercise book with 'TASTE' written in capital letters on the cover. The whole history of the group had been set down in it step by step: the first photos, press cuttings, drawings, comments, tickets, concert flyers and souvenirs, and now another new page had to be turned. He carefully put the book back in its place alongside his other souvenirs collected over the years, including a portrait of Buddy Holly that Rory had painted, aged twelve (on the back of a Kellogg's cornflakes box). Painting was just another of Rory's talents; he had attended evening courses at art school.

Putting aside the recent upheavals, Rory thought about the way forward. Music was his entire life, and although he now had a dazzling mastery of the guitar and a large reputation, he was not satisfied. In his own eyes, the ultimate objectives that he had set himself were still a long way off. He was aware that he still had it in him to push the limits of his art much further, that he could not yet veer away from the task of learning, persevering, living – and overcoming the inevitable disappointments. In other words, there was more

suffering to come. He was conscious of this and was ready for it, ready to take any blows on the chin, preserving his winning smile and kindness, while showing the world that he was strong and could give as good as he got if that was what it took to get where he wanted.

*Buddy Holly painted by Rory, aged 12*

Rory was forever on the lookout for new discoveries, new ways of improving his guitar technique. He would study the links between different styles, like country music, folk and blues – especially the blues. It was the one type of music that really got to him, that moved him, with which he was obsessed above all others. He would spend long hours examining, analysing and adapting this music in all its different facets, from Louisiana Swamp blues, to boogie-woogie blues, to Mississippi Delta blues: each of them fascinated him. He reproduced the music of his masters, lovingly preserving the spirit, originality and essence of 1920s and 1930s blues. He paid homage to Eddie 'Son' House, recognised as the father of the Delta Blues, and to Charley Patton, who had, in turn, influenced Robert Johnson, himself highly respected by fellow 'bottleneckers' Eric Clapton and Jimmy Page.

He worshipped Blind Boy Fuller's ragtime and Piemont blues styles, as well as John Lee 'Sonny Boy' Williamson – who had introduced the harmonica into Chicago blues – Big Bill Bronzy, Leadbelly – the folk–blues artist and writer of 'Good Night Irene' – not forgetting Muddy Waters, Chuck Berry and Lonnie Donegan. They all had an undeniable influence on the music Rory created; he did not imitate them, however, but merely conscientiously studied and learnt the lessons of the masters. These people would soon come to recognise Rory's talent and welcome him as one of their own.

Away from the bustle of London and the artificial whirlwind of its show-business scene – which he would never get used to – Rory worked on his music, slowly building it up into a solid mix of gut feeling, human warmth, experience, curiosity and will-power, giving of himself for the enjoyment of others. He increasingly wrote his own lyrics too, fuelled by his eager observations of life around him, by an intrinsic need to push his understanding of it further, to make new discoveries, to innovate. Inspired by his life, his imagination, his passions and his sufferings, his texts reflected everything that attracted his curiosity about life. He adored the cinema, for example, and knew the films of his favourite actors, like Lino Ventura (*Le Silencieux*), almost by heart, intrigued by the man behind the mask, the hard man with a heart of gold, genuine, loyal and undyingly faithful to his true friends.

Rory was also an avid reader of detective novels and would later dedicate the track 'Continental Op' to the American writer Dashiell Hammett, one of the originators of the 'hard-boiled genre' who, in the 1920s, wrote stories whose heroes were 'real' people with depth and weaknesses: losers who were often left with only one thing intact – the pureness of their souls. Rory shared Hammett's sense of precision and description: his songs were always like stories. He loved characters played by actors such as Humphrey Bogart, who could still look themselves in the mirror at the end of the day, rebels of their era and of history, as in the history of his own beloved Ireland. He loved the quality of writing in novels such as *The Maltese Falcon* and the authenticity of such characters as the private dicks of the Continental Detective Agency in San Francisco.

Rory had finally found his musical voice, with its own peculiar tone: at times warm and innately sensual, sometimes rough and aggressive, always distinctive. Without having to force it, he wrapped his voice around the words and the words around his music, insinuating, imitating and combining perfectly his guitar style with his vocals. Fusing the notes together, he intertwined the different sounds, superimposing one on top of another in absolute synchronisation, producing harmonies that melted into each other. Rory's ambition was simply to produce the music that he liked and to share the joys and heartbreak that it brought him with anyone who would care to listen. He had no interest whatsoever in prancing around at the top of the charts. This was the golden rule from which he was never to waver all his life: he would play no part in the ephemeral glory of 'superstardom'.

Brian May, Queen's young guitarist, was a fervent admirer of Rory. This brilliant student, decorated with degrees and diplomas, also frequented the Marquee, to see Taste, where he would bump into Rory. They struck a chord, and a friendship began to grow. Queen and Taste lived in the same neighbourhood for a certain time, and indeed Queen's first gig with Freddie Mercury as vocalist was a support slot at an early Rory Gallagher gig in Dunstable Technical College, north of London. After Rory's death, Brian May closeted himself in a studio and recorded some of Rory's tracks, as a last homage to his friend.

Jimmy Page was another acquaintance of Rory's. Led Zeppelin had begun life under the name of the New Yardbirds and were often on the same bill as Taste.

So by 1968, backed by John Wilson and Richard McCracken, Rory was moving ever closer to the blues of Muddy Waters, Buddy Guy, Willie Dixon and Lemon Jefferson. He was developing his own particular style, coloured by both blues and rock. Although his new musical partners had been more or less imposed upon him, they were, nevertheless, injecting new life and energy into Taste, producing a unique sort of progressive blues that set them apart from other groups. They had once more started attracting the attention of London, where the originality of their sound and the talent and individuality of the musicians was greeted with acclaim. As a result, the studio was calling them again.

The first of the trio's four albums was simply called *Taste*. The whole range of their work at that time was covered in nine tracks, each carrying Rory's distinctive mark. The album alternates blues numbers ('Leaving Blues'), traditional numbers ('Sugar Mama', 'Catfish'), 'rock and blues' ('Blister on the Moon'), acoustic numbers ('Hail') and a reference to the origins of rock and roll in a homage to the country artist Hank Snow ('I'm Moving On'). Rory's guitar is lively throughout and the phrasing precise, with very few special effects, underlined by subtle interplays with the vocals ('Same Old Story'), breaks and beautiful soaring solos, underpinned by a solid bass foundation. *Taste* is a studio album which, but for the absence of crowd noise, exudes the energy of the live performance.

*Queen album given to Rory by Brian May*

# Mr O'Driscoll

Rory was slumped in a chair staring at the floor, his long hair hanging down over his forlorn face. While the Dublin police were filling in their report, Donal and the others tried, in vain, to console him, but to no avail: Rory was silently seething rage. After the concert, the band had loaded all their equipment into the van before taking part in a press interview and then going for something to eat. They had returned to the van to find that it had been broken into and Rory's beloved Fender had been stolen, kidnapped! So devastated, so depressed was Rory that they were all determined to move heaven and earth in an effort to recover the missing guitar. At that time, there was still only one television channel in the Republic, it ran a regular programme called *Garda Patrol*, on which lost-and-found appeals were broadcast to help the police locate stolen property.

'As I'm sure you can imagine,' announced the officer in a rather mocking tone, 'our unfortunate musician is somewhat distraught by the loss of his instrument, although it must be said that it might be better all round if he didn't get it back, considering the noise he's been making with it!' The joke soon did the rounds, and by the next day the whole population knew about it. The thief found himself left with no alternative but to abandon the 'hot' guitar where it was sure to be found, in the knowledge that it had become unsellable overnight. So Rory got his Stratocaster – and his smile – back, and from that moment on never let it out of his sight, entrusting it only when necessary to Donal and later to his faithful friend and roadie Tom O'Driscoll.

Originally from a little village called Schull just outside Cork, O'Driscoll went to a Fontana concert at the age of fifteen. He was taken with the young guitarist – his style, ability and kindness. Tom was an immediate fan, and followed the group on their tours. He left his home village and moved to Cork city, in order to be nearer to the group, sometimes sleeping under bridges as he waited for their next concert. He appears in a photograph from that time, standing just behind the guitarist, who is playing and at the same time

*Tom O'Driscoll*

leaning towards him and talking into his ear. The guitarist of course is Rory. A lifelong friendship was born. Hard-working, willing, capable, Tom soon became indispensable. In 1973, the moment came when, logically, he became part of the next picture: the Rory Gallagher Band. Tom O'Driscoll was to accompany Rory across the globe, and his efficiency undoubtedly added to the success of Rory's concerts.

Tom ensured the smooth running of more than 200 concerts a year, and for more than five years had no real home or fixed abode. He was constantly on the road, sacrificing his private life to serve Rory and his music with dedication. Rory had such charisma that all who met him were won over by him, were touched by him and remained faithful to him. All this happened naturally, for Rory always went straight to the heart of things. There was no pretence, only honesty and authenticity.

# PIBLOKTO

Although not in uniform, everyone knew that Marc Hélin was in the middle of his national service: the haircut was the give-away. As usual when he was home on leave, Marc was clearly half-drunk already. Leaning on the bar with a pint in his hand, swaying slightly and gesticulating, he would tell the same old stories over and over again to whoever was willing to listen. Well-liked by the regulars despite his cracked taste in records, he would quite often be bought a beer and led over to the pinball machine, the only place where he was likely to put his drink down for a moment. His preferred poison was Champi lager: 'The Queen of Beers for the King of Fools!' he would chortle every time he ordered another, which was often! ·

Back at the pinball machine, he hung onto the corners of the machine as his eyes attempted to follow the trajectory of the small, metal marble coming towards him, and then with a surprisingly deft flick of his wrist he sent it hurtling into one of the pins, setting the scoreboard spinning. 'D'yer see that lads, champion!' he exclaimed, as he raised his glass to his lips and emptied it in one gulp. It was at that moment that Noeghan Jelcoe entered the Wattrelos bar, which he considered his local. Aptly named *Aux Amis* (The Friendship Inn) by the landlord, Lucien, it was for him and many others a haven where he could always be sure to come across a familiar face. Marc's face lit up as he noticed Noeghan come in, and he staggered, smiling, over to greet him, clutching his empty glass, which Noeghan obligingly offered to refill. 'Yous'll never guess where I just bin ... ' Marc began, 'only t'see Taste is all, wiv McCracken an' Wilson ... none o' yer old Gallagher Band it weren't ... in Dourges they was playin' ... "What's Going On?" "Sugar Mama" an' all that, great!' To illustrate his point, he tipped half his pint on the floor while mimicking Rory on his guitar and emitting onomatopoeic belches supposedly reproducing the sounds of the notes. 'All the way to the Piblokto on shanks's pony I went just t'see 'im, forty kilometres there and as many back. It were magic. Pity yer missed it, Rory singing "Catfish" an' all!' And with that, his eyes began to water and he burst into tears.

Around the time of Marc's marathon walk to Dourges, the music venues in the north of France were disappearing one after the other. The Twenty Club in Mouscron had closed its doors, and many others had become discos. The one exception was the Ram Dam in Dourges. Albert Warin, the former schoolteacher, still did not have a telephone in his own house, but his club was as popular and sought after as ever, attracting crowds of youngsters thirsting to discover the new bands that were eager to play in front of such avid audiences. All calls from London were put through to Mario's house, where his ageing mother, whose French left a lot to be desired, would often be the one to pick up the phone. She had no problem, however, understanding what the English voices wanted and, laying the receiver beside the phone, would hurry next door to knock on the door. Albert would put his corrections to one side and run around to take the call and negotiate an agreement in broken English. Most Friday evenings he was to be seen at the station in Arras picking up artists like Kevyn Ayers (who had the advantage of speaking French) or Pete Brown (Jack Bruce's – and therefore Cream's – lyricist), who was to become a regular at the club, appreciated to the point that the Ram Dam was renamed the Piblokto after his group.

One particular night after a concert, the club was broken into and Pete's bongos were stolen. Upset but resigned, he set off to Arras without his treasured instruments. Some of the club's regulars were so incensed by and ashamed of this black mark on the reputation of their town, however, that they decided to do a bit of investigating. Dourges being a small mining community, they had little trouble in locating the perpetrator of the crime, and a group of some of the larger residents went to pay him a visit. Dragged from his bed, the thief quickly indicated to his interrogators that the bongos were to be found in his father's shed at the end of the garden. The vigilantes quickly snatched the drums from their hiding place and made a beeline for the railway station, arriving there just as the train was about to leave. Hearing his named called from the platform, Pete, already settled despondently into his compartment, put his head out of the window to see five or six beefy lads charging after the train shouting their heads off. He hurried to the door just in time to recover his instruments before the train disappeared down the track. The honour of the club had been saved.

Leaning over the map, someone pointed out Dourges to Rory and Donal: a barely visible little spot in the mining area of the north of France near the Belgian border, not far from Lille. Making note of any landmarks along the way, they carefully worked out a route taking them through Arras and Lens. Luckily, Dourges wasn't far off the motorway!

At the end of a tiring journey in the van, Taste disembarked in the heartland of the terraced house to be greeted, much to their surprise, as the messiahs of good music. Several young fans were on hand to guide them into the main concert hall, where the promoter, Albert Warin, hurried over to welcome them.

Rory's hair fell across his doll-like face, to cover the collar of his denim jacket, as he nodded gratefully in accepting the chair that had been offered to him and sat down at a table laden with coffee cups. Albert's lively, dark-haired wife, Simone, gestured to the four lads to help themselves. Rory murmured a polite *merci* as he lifted a steaming cup to his parched lips. For the second time on a tour to the Continent, his brother Donal was by his side acting as road manager, taking the organisational load off Rory's shoulders and sorting out any problems that might arise – taking charge of the driving, overseeing contracts, negotiating with the agent in London who had booked Taste and advising Rory on the recording deals that were starting to materialise.

At that moment, a small blonde girl, hardly old enough to walk, came into the room, whimpering. 'This is my daughter, Aurore,' said Simone as she took the little girl up into her arms. Smiling and holding out his hand to her, Rory repeated each syllable of her name to himself: 'Au-ro-re, that's a nice name.' Albert was delighted to discover that this rising star was such a nice, gentle human being. Rory, meanwhile, felt flattered by the genuine hospitality of this club owner in immediately welcoming them into his home, even though they had only just met. They both smiled as their eyes met across the table and Albert, pouring them each a drop of stronger stuff that he had produced from nowhere, proposed a toast. 'To the concert,' he said, as he brought his glass up to meet those of the others around the table. 'Cheers,' replied Rory, still smiling.

Shortly afterwards, Donal asked to see the hall. There was still the equipment to be set up, sound checks to be done and, most important of all, the difference in wattage of the electricity supply to be sorted out. They were going to have to rig up some system to convert the 110-volt amps to the 220-volt mains supply to avoid blowing the whole lot. As he got up from the table with the others, Rory paused to thank Simone, who would for evermore fondly remember this 'charming young man'.

A few chords were all it took to set the Piblokto alight that evening. The audience was instantly transfixed, completely under Taste's spell from the outset, electrified by Rory's blues, paralysed by his acoustic technique, entranced by his rock and blues. Later that night, Rory and the others, accompanied by Albert and a few close friends, were eating a pizza in the cafeteria that Albert had opened up in a corner of the club to help bolster the floundering takings. It was Mario, in fact, who had taken on the catering. The shared meal was to put the seal on a blossoming friendship between the members of Taste and the owners of the club. Taste were to become a regular fixture there. Every time they came to play, they would do five or six shows during the course of a weekend: in one of the bars at lunchtime, a matinée performance in the Piblokto, a repeat performance in one of the neighbouring clubs a little later in the day, followed by a further evening spot in Dourges. One Sunday in particular, while playing in a place near Arras, they were even asked to play a tango or two! Despite the difficult conditions, Rory always had fond memories of the period, largely because of the incredible atmosphere that had reigned in the Piblokto. The club was to close in the 1970s, leaving Albert Warin so weighed down by debts that the loan repayments were automatically docked from his teacher's salary. In the face of such adversity, however, he refused to throw in the towel and gradually fought back, forging a reputation for himself as one of the foremost tour organisers in the north of France, working with acts such as Pink Floyd, Frank Zappa, the Grateful Dead, Status Quo, Bob Marley and many more, including, of course, Taste and Rory Gallagher during a friendship that was to last twenty-five years, until the last of Rory's gigs in the north of France in October 1994. At this gig, the young blonde woman who was to fill in for Albert, pay Donal and take Rory and his entourage to dinner would be none other than Aurore, Albert and Simone's daughter.

# ALTO SAX

Although the band was playing a great many gigs, the receipts were hardly enough for the Gallagher brothers, Wilson and McCracken to get by on, much less get rich on. The royalties from the first album could not be relied upon for that either. Nevertheless, Polydor, under the management of Eddie Kennedy, began to consider the possibility of making a follow-up LP. To this end, Taste set up a base in London, with Rory and Donal sharing a single-room bedsit in a building where noise was strictly prohibited. Apparently oblivious to the rudimentary nature of his lodgings, Rory shut himself in for hours on end, completely submerged in his new passion, the saxophone. Getting inspiration and teaching from the records of Django Reinhardt, Ornette Coleman, John Coltrane and the artists of the Vanguard and Blue Note labels, Rory became increasingly absorbed by everything that jazz and its essence signified; by how it was constructed, how it was played, how it could be lived and breathed, by its freedom.

This fascination had first been sparked off when Rory met Captain Beefheart in 1967 at Taste's first concert in Britain, at Nottingham, where the band were paid the princely sum of five pounds. Captain Beefheart – as Don Van Vliet, a friend of Frank Zappa's, was known at the time – was on the same bill as them, and all the musicians were sharing the same backstage dressing-room. Rory and Captain Beefheart had talked for hours about music, jazz and improvisation, with Beefheart admitting to Rory that he really didn't care one way or the other if he played a few false notes: 'the more the better', as he said. Rory had had trouble accepting this concept: it went against the grain of his self-taught musical culture. His experience with the showbands had rather instilled in him an unbending musical discipline where nothing was left to chance, everything was calculated, down to the last quaver and crochet, and the music was fine-tuned to the last semitone. His instinct was increasingly telling him, however, that such strait-jackets were not necessarily the way he would produce his best music, that he should find a means of liberating himself and letting impulse and desire have a freer reign in his creative process. This conversation gave voice to nagging doubts and led him more than willingly towards the idea of improvisation, and thus to the adventure of jazz.

Donal was surprised to learn that Rory had spent so much money on a Selmer alto sax, along with the 'tune a day' method to teach himself how to play. If push had come to shove, Donal could have understood Rory buying another guitar, despite the band's dire financial situation, but a saxophone! What in heaven's name had possessed him now! But Rory persevered and conscientiously set about the task of mastering it. He practised for days on end and made remarkable progress, picking up breathing and embouchure techniques as if they were the most natural things in the world. After just a few weeks, he had progressed beyond the book-method and into improvisation. To avoid the grumbling of the landlord about the noise, he shut himself inside the bedsit's one wardrobe, pushing aside the clothes and practising, perfecting his technique until he was satisfied with the resulting peculiar, personal sound he managed to produce. The effects were astounding. Helped by the confined conditions in which he worked and the acoustic-deadening quality of the clothes around him, he gradually sculpted a smooth, silky, satiny sound of a rare, subdued quality that resonated solitude and blissful sadness.

Both McCracken and Wilson were taken with this new departure and the influences quickly made themselves felt in the new recording sessions that Taste 2 were undertaking. The album was to include rasping rock-and-blues numbers like the classic 'What's Going On?', harmonica touches, as in 'If the Day Was Any Longer', delicate acoustic guitar sequences that classical guitarist Brassens would have approved of, such as in 'See Here', and the surprising, moving 'I'll Remember', where voice and guitar melt gloriously into one. The album was to be called *On the Boards*, the title-track featuring a sensitive, emotional, disconcerting saxophone line that had a magic quality all its own. The jazz influence was also to be felt in the guitar-playing on tracks such as 'It's Happened Before, It'll Happen Again', which has echoes of René Thomas – a downbeat, 1950s to 1960s style of jazz that conjured up images of black-and-white detective films. Rory was to say towards the end of his life that he would have liked to try writing a film score. In a way, he already had.

During an interview in the *New Musical Express* in 1969, John Lennon, hardly a novice in the world of music at the time, was quoted as saying that the music he was listening to the most was that of a group who went by the name of Taste. Indeed the public at large seem to confirm Lennon's declared admiration for this group of musicians, who were without pretension but eminently genuine, not a 'supergroup', as was in vogue at the time, but simply a superb band. The descriptions of the musicians that were circulated by word of mouth were bordering on caricature. The popularity of the long-haired solo guitarist in his trainers, crumpled jeans and checked

*Programme announcements*

shirts had started to spread beyond the confines of the inner circle of the music business. There was no fooling the general public, the authentic paying fans who turned out from Cork to Dourges, from Belfast to London and from Hamburg to Montreux to acclaim their group, who were never more at ease than on stage, in front of their supporters – as the album *Live in Montreux*, recorded at the jazz festival there, illustrates perfectly. Roddy Doyle was later drawn to this story, perhaps using it as the inspiration for the film *The Commitments*; indeed he even proposed that Rory play a principal role in it – that of Rory Dean!

Rory was overjoyed as Donal held the piece of paper aloft for all to see. Taste were to play support for Blind Faith (Eric Clapton, Ginger Baker, Rick Gretch and Stevie Winwood) on their tour of Canada and the United States! The tour was to last several weeks, criss-crossing the North American continent, with other groups like Delanney and Bonnie in support. They were all to travel in the same enormous bus, which would be an ideal breeding ground for contacts and exchanges, and indeed it proved to be the birthplace of the mutual respect and admiration that was to grow up between Clapton and Gallagher. For Rory it was also the chance to discover first-hand the different corners of the country where the music that he loved originated, and to meet its foremost proponents on their own territory – legends from whom he could learn, progress and discover.

In New York the whole tour party turned up in a small club one night to celebrate Muddy Waters, who was playing several nights there in front of a small, select audience. It was 1969. That evening Eric Clapton, Leon Russell, Stevie Winwood, Delanney Bramlett, Rory and many others paid homage to Muddy Waters. During the next three days, Muddy Waters surrounded himself with his 'family' and was honoured by his 'spiritual children' in a succession of improvised jam sessions in which many greats, such as Jimi Hendrix and Buddy Miles, also participated. It is impossible to state with any degree of certainty that Rory and Hendrix played together on the same stage at the same time during this improvised, euphoric festival in honour

*Isle of Wight programme 1970*

of Waters, but it is far from inconceivable that the two men, one left- and the other right-handed, crossed guitars on that occasion. If it did happen, it must have been a truly memorable occasion.

Rory had immense respect for Hendrix. Their paths were to cross many times in the streets, record and music shops of London. Jimi is known to have attended a Taste concert in Blaises in south Kensington, to have played within the select confines of the University of Belfast, and they shared the same bill at several festivals, including the Woburn Music Festival at Bedford in England on 6 and 7 July 1968, and the

44

Isle of Wight in 1970. Although never programmed on the same day, the two men met and made contact – but very few details are known about what went on between them. What is known is that Rory admired what Jimi had done to push back the frontiers of the blues from their humble beginnings in the ghettos of the United States. Rory was genuinely saddened to learn of Hendrix's death. It had been one of Rory's childhood friends, Jerry Osbourne, who had taken the famous shot of Jimi going up the stairs onto the stage in Denmark for what was to prove to be the last time. An ultimate ascension that many have taken as symbolising or foreshadowing his imminent ascension to heaven!

# ROLAND

Jo Dekmine – a friend of Julian Beck's (Living Theatre) and of Léo Ferré, who had also discovered, amongst others, Mamma from New York, Bread and Puppet Theatre while also running the well-known venue Theatre 140 in Brussels – launched the Musique Aujourd'hui (Today's Music) movement, which was to bring the unknown Pink Floyd to Belgium. The festival that he organised in June of that year in Antwerp, called the Pop Event, was a great success, and it was Noeghan who found himself up on stage introducing the acts in French to a predominantly Flemish audience. And they weren't just any acts either, but heavyweights such as Yes, Nice, Colosseum, Fleetwood Mac, Chicken Shack and a Belgian blues-and-rock combo known as the Blues Workshop led by a musician called Roland Van Campenout. He was a well-loved, well-respected character on the Dutch music scene who had learnt the tricks of the trade with some of the mythical figures of the folk-and-blues world. Starting his career with Derroll Adams as a stage and session guitarist, he had become friends with Ferré Grignard, who had taken him around all the music-soaked clubs and bars of Antwerp, such as De Muse. With the insolent ease that comes from true talent, Roland had quickly risen in the ranks of blues, folk and rock music, with even a few forays into the world of jazz.

Noeghan was a freelance journalist, a sort of reporter-cum-roadie, not always recognised by the so-called 'music' establishment. He had cut his teeth in 1967 on the *Disco Revue* before participating in the creation of *Rock and Folk* and then *Best* magazine. During the events of 1968, he had his radio baptism on RTB (a

Belgian radio station). Although Noeghan didn't yet know Roland, the two men later discovered that they were both involved in the same project, Radio Concorde. This was planned as a European pirate station which, in 1968, would have been transmitted in several languages from a boat anchored off the coast of the Netherlands. The project never saw the light of day, for mysterious financial or political reasons, although Noeghan and Roland each separately spent several days on board testing the equipment.

It was during the Pop Event that Jo Dekmine started considering the idea of organising a similar rock festival in Paris itself. Noeghan was sent off with a mission: to contact Jean Georgakarakos, a close associate of Pierre Barouh's, to see what he thought of getting it off the ground. Sitting on a terrace café on Avenue Friedland, Noeghan was telling Georgakarakos all about it between bites of croissant and sips of coffee. On hearing the story, the record dealer, with his customary impetuosity, blurted out 'Let's do it!' In his enthusiasm to get the project off the ground, Georgakarakos had the idea of buying outright the jazz magazine *Actuel* and creating the Byg record label, thus signing up all the free jazz artists who were participating in the Pan African Festival in Algiers to do a compilation album entitled *Actuel,* including work by artists such as Graham Montcur, Art Ensemble of Chicago and Dave Burell.

As all these artists passed through the office on Avenue Friedland, Noeghan set about establishing the rock side of the programme. His idea was to put the festival, designed to be a mixture of rock, free jazz and contemporary music, on at the Baltard de Halles de Paris pavilions, which was semi-abandoned at the time. After months of deliberation, the Paris authorities at the town hall opposed the idea of the Halles becoming a cultural venue. Future administrations would, however, see the light on this issue. Numerous misadventures later, the festival was banned entirely from French soil, and eventually took place in a field at Amougies in Belgium, in October 1969. On the bill were names like Frank Zappa, Ten Years After, Soft Machine, Pink Floyd, Captain Beefheart, Alexis Korner, Fat Mattress – a lineup to rival the billings of the Woodstock and Isle of Wight festivals that were to take place that same year.

# AACHEN

The sound of the tyres on the tarmac came to Noeghan through the open window of the BMW as he sped down the motorway, foot to the floor, listening absent-mindedly to a Belgian passenger that he had picked up as arranged in front of the RTB building on Place Flagey, Brussels. The man was an unknown, music-mad student and avid listener to the 'Formula J' radio broadcast, which was very popular in Belgium and the north of France at the time.

July 1970 was an exceptionally hot month, and the rock festivals were looking to be so as well. For Noeghan's passenger, to get a lift to Aix La Chapelle was a godsend. The lift had been arranged through a system of organised hitch-hiking organised by Formule J, saving money for car-owners and time and energy for non-car-owners. Before picking up his travelling companion, who was full of praise for the group Taste, Noeghan had called into the office to get a Nagra recorder. Aix la Chapelle was the second music festival that he had covered for RTB, the first having been in Rotterdam the previous week. In the weeks to follow, he was to cover festivals at Aix en Provence, Biot and the Isle of Wight.

During the festival, Noeghan was introduced to one of the organisers who helped him be accepted backstage and allowed him to meet groups such as Hardyn and York, the Spencer Davis Band, Edgar Broughton and Pink Floyd, whom he had previously encountered at Theatre 140. He found David Gilmour sunbathing anonymously in the middle of the crowd. They talked about music and cinema, because Pink Floyd had recently produced the soundtrack to two films: Barbet Schroeder's *More* and Michelangelo Antonioni's *Zabriskie Point*. Gilmour explained to Noeghan the difference between the making of the two soundtracks. For the first, 'It was funny, we did it so quickly, instinctively, in a matter of a few days,' Gilmour said. 'We wrote and recorded the lot in eight days. Schroeder gave us a free hand, whereas it was different with Antonioni. He had very precise ideas about what he wanted and would regularly come to the studio to set out exactly what he wanted from us.'

Meanwhile, on stage, Richie Blackmore was in the process of slamming the neck of his guitar into one of the spotlights, which shattered in an explosion of glass splinters. As they watched, he set fire to an amp and flames shot up around the speakers. Deep Purple's music was a mixture of hard rock punctuated by moments of intense calm, featuring the keyboards of John Lord, the piercing voice of Ian Gillian, and the drumming of Ian Pace, with Roger Glover on the bass. The minds of the thousands of spectators from Germany, Holland, Belgium and France were blown away by Deep Purple. Following them, on the other podium set up to cut out the waiting time between groups, If took over, with their swinging jazz-rock. Noeghan had previously seen them at the Piblokto in Dourges, but what really made this event unforgettable for Noeghan was his discovery, in this bucolic setting, of the group Taste. Unbeknown to him, the group was an institution in Germany and the audience here had already been converted to the fierce, to-the-point, no-frills blues of Rory Gallagher, which worked its way under your skin to whisper to your soul, with no need for artificial effects. Noeghan made some live recordings of the concert and did a short interview with Rory. Polite, swift, professional, anonymous contact was established, followed by an exchange of smiles and handshakes.

## ISLE OF WIGHT

For the festival of all festivals on the Isle of Wight at the end of August, Noeghan set off with Jacques Barsamian, from *Pop Music* magazine, and Jacques Vassal, from *Rock and Folk*. In order to avoid the rush – 300,000 people were headed towards the island – the three of them made a few detours. They parked the BMW by the port just opposite the Isle of Wight and crossed the bay by hovercraft, mingling with the long procession of the faithful. At the ticket desk, it was a real free-for-all. 'It's sold out,' someone confirmed. 'There are no more places left inside the grounds.' Barsamian, Noeghan and the others climbed up the adjacent hill. Regularly, around the backstage area, they would get a rundown of the situation from DJs, Jouffa, from Europe 1, and Hebey, from RTL radio. 'I can give you the Baez interview if you're interested,' one of the DJs said. They were, and took a copy, Noeghan sending a newsflash to Brussels. For three days and three nights, Noeghan never let his Nagra recorder out of his sight. He ate with it beside him, and even slept on the grass with it strapped to his shoulder.

The Hell's Angels were out in force, in leather, chains and cudgels. As Noeghan moved up the hill, they were making their way down. He started to get worried about his equipment, but they took no notice of it. He then decided to follow them. There were about a hundred of them in a threatening semicircle facing a group of stoical, emotionless policemen, who stood with both hands gripping their truncheons. Words were exchanged in a bitter tone, as the atmosphere became tenser. The authorities and the gang leaders came to a last-minute compromise. The Hell's Angels dispersed, and confrontation was avoided. The photographers, who had gathered in the hope of getting a good picture or two, moved away disappointedly.

However, there were still grounds for complaint. Plain-clothes policemen with dogs were holding

*First page of the Isle of Wight programme 1970*

back some youths who were trying to force their way onto the festival grounds. People were speaking up, moaning about money. Some kids were taking drugs, one guy fell off the cliff, and there were no doors on the toilets. The Isle of Wight line-up was impressive: the Doors, Emerson Lake and Palmer, Ten Years After, the Who, Cactus, Chicago, Family, Tony Joe White, Free, Procol Harum, Mungo Jerry, Joni Mitchell, John Sebastian, Tiny Tim, Arrival, Spirit, Miles Davis, Lighthouse, Donovan, the Moody Blues, Leonard Cohen, the Pentangle, Richie Havens, Jethro Tull, the Everly Brothers, Redbone, Kris Kristofferson, Joan Baez, Heaven, Kathy Smith, Ralph McTell, Jimi Hendrix, Taste.

Rory felt dizzy as he set foot on the huge stage. Under a blazing sun, he could see a surging, multicoloured tide of people which trembled, shifted, swayed and cried. Rory's two eyes were met by some six hundred thousand eyes glued to him and his band members as they arrived on stage. McCracken plugged his bass into his orange amp; Wilson toyed with his drumsticks and tested the foot pedal of his bass drum. Flashing a toothy grin, with his long mane of hair falling over his checked shirt and jeans, Rory tuned his guitar and struck his first notes, looking totally in control.

In their own inimitable way, with no frills or excess, Taste impressed their public with their gutsy, heartfelt, solid, down-to-earth music. Their tracks were long, with numbers such as 'Sugar Mama' and 'I Feel So Good' lasting up to ten minutes. Their version of 'Catfish' lasted a full fourteen minutes.

Cameras hovered around Rory, but he couldn't see them, aware only of the hill on the horizon, dropping straight to the sea, and the crowd, a human swell tossing and pitching to the rhythm of the music he poured over them.

The critics were very impressed, and wrote about Taste for the first time, and the public too were left in no doubt about the band's talents. When Taste left the stage, the crowd cried out for more. Backstage, Rory had already returned to the grey Ford van parked beside the platform. The loudspeakers were calling him back and the cameras came looking for him. Rory, John and Richard reappeared, to the roaring clamour of the crowd. There were five encores, all of which was heartening for Rory on stage, his face glowing, radiating an intense inner joy. Sometimes, however, a fleeting shadow of doubt seemed to cross his face, revealing underlying tension.

Dissent had been rising within the group for some while, due to management problems as well as musical differences. What finally

*Photos illustrating the LP and CD 'Taste, Live at the Isle of Wight'*

brought things to a head was Rory's request to see the manager's accounts. On a musical front, John Wilson would have liked to continue in the same vein and take the experience further, carrying Rory closer to free form music, and although Rory was more than happy to experiment with this musical genre, he refused to dedicate himself to it totally.

After *On the Boards*, Rory decided that the band members had reached the limit of the potential such music could generate within the framework of Taste. He preferred instead to give more prominence to the blues, and to devote himself to his guitar. He didn't want to spread himself too thinly. Wilson was still in favour of a freer orientation. Conflict was therefore inevitable, and the situation became difficult. The drummer refused to play certain numbers which he considered too bluesy or too basic. Rory put up with this, but reluctantly.

Taste split following the Isle of Wight gig but following intervention by Polydor, Rory agreed to complete a sell out European tour. The final concert was at Queens University on 31 December 1970. With their manager, Eddie Kennedy, Wilson and McCracken formed Stud. Rory was sorely tried by this affair, declaring himself exhausted and numb, with nothing left to give. The press attacked him, making him out to be responsible for the split and to have become some sort of dictator. Rory was wounded and hurt by all this. From that moment on, and for some time to come, he would refuse to play any Taste tracks on stage, forcing himself to forget, in an effort to erase the hurt from his memory. But he remained sensitive to any attacks on the subject, having suffered enough. The manager from this period has since died. Many years afterwards John Wilson telephoned Rory. It was perhaps from that moment on that Rory entertained the idea of playing one or two of the old Taste songs again for the sheer pleasure of it. The songs were his, he wrote them; some of them were good, some of them were classics, but Rory was never one for living in the past. He had kept this heartfelt pain hidden within himself for almost twenty years, not wanting to sour things. But when the others came forward to contact him again, he was undeniably relieved.

# RORY GALLAGHER AND HIS BAND

Donal worked for a short period as tour manager for Atomic Rooster. Rory meanwhile wrote material for his first solo album, produced under his own name. His first step was to put together a group, a trio. He recruited a bass player, telephoning Gerry McAvoy from Belfast, whose group Deep Joy had just split up. In 1967, Gerry had run into Rory in Crimble's music shop on the Dublin Road in Belfast. In McAvoy's eyes, Rory was already a star, as Taste's lead guitarist – a man with whom young musicians dreamt of playing.

Gerry was only fifteen, but he already had his own band, with a mate, Brendan O'Neill, on drums. Rory was browsing in the shop, but Gerry was there with a mission: to buy his first bass guitar for sixty pounds. Together, they spent two hours chatting in the shop. Gerry's group, Deep Joy, had played with Taste in Northern Ireland in 1968 and 1969, and again when they had been in England. So Gerry and Rory knew each other. Gerry had started out not as a bass player but as a lead guitarist. After some internal changes in his old group, he had swapped his guitar for a bass, and never looked back. Deep Joy moved to London in 1970, but Brendan did not follow. His girlfriend had given him an ultimatum: choose either her or his music. For a while, Brendan chose her, working in a factory. Wilgar Campbell, a young Irish musician from a group called the Method, was his replacement. When Deep Joy split up, Gerry didn't hesitate when Rory suggested that he join him; this marked the beginning of a close friendship that was to last twenty years.

The typical Irish musician, Gerry's influences were deeply rooted in his family. His mother was a singer; his father played the harmonica. In the 1930s, his grandfather had played mandolin with a group that had toured throughout the country. Unsurprisingly, Gerry was a blues fanatic. John Mayall and the Bluesbreakers had first got him interested in it, and he had also been greatly influenced by Muddy Waters. Gerry was outwardly calm, reserved and self-effacing, and adept at martial arts. With remarkable realism and self-control, he became attached to Rory – allowing him to make considerable progress in terms of musical maturity. Gerry's role was a crucial one. His solid, heavy, powerful bass-playing, executed with all the style of a lead guitarist, fitted perfectly with Rory's musical vision. The arrival of Wilgar Campbell, on drums, completed the transformation. He was an ideal addition to the line-up.

*Rory Gallagher,* recorded in London in 1971 at the Advision Studios, was Rory's first solo album. Memories of Taste were still in the air, however. The sound engineer, Eddy Offord, had worked with Rory on *On the Boards.* The first track on the new album, 'Laundromat', featuring Rory's explosive guitar riffs, had been written around the time of Taste's separation, when the group were living together in a bedsit in Earl's Court in London. On 'Hands Up', Rory was trying to blast away all the resentment he felt following Taste's split. On 'For the Last Time', he goes back over the difficulties that he had to tolerate during the band's break-up. But these were only a few of the themes Rory was exploring, drawing inspiration from everyday life. Music for him was simply a reflection of reality, an expression of life's struggles. On a technical level, 'Sinner Boy' revealed a fantastic slide-guitar technique. Even at the age of twenty-three, Rory showed total mastery of his Telecaster. The track was very special to him, for personal, intimate reasons: it dealt with the theme of alcohol in much the same way as Woodie Guthrie had. The mandolin, an instrument he had only just taken up, makes an appearance on 'It's You'. 'Just the Smile' is a sideways glance in the direction of the Pentangle, a folk group from the 1960s and 1970s, for whose guitarist, Bert Jansch, Rory had great respect and affection.

For the first time, Rory featured a piano on his recordings. Vincent Crane, the keyboard player from Atomic Rooster, was brought in for two tracks, at Donal's instigation. On 'Wave Myself Goodbye', there is a heavenly dialogue between piano and acoustic guitar, whereas on 'I'm Not Surprised', the keyboards are much more energetic, 'Delivering a Fats Domino-style accompaniment to Rory's raucous guitar riffs,' says Donal.

Rory plays alto saxophone on 'Can't Believe It's True', revealing the influence jazz had upon him, and his admiration for John Coltrane and Eric Dolphy. Guitar and alto saxophone were double-tracked, creating a spellbinding combination of Rory's talents. Rory also paid homage to two blues players close to his heart by interpreting Muddy Waters' 'Gypsy Woman' and 'It Takes Time', which had originally been recorded by premier Chicago blues guitarist Otis Rush.

*Rory Gallagher* was the first album produced by Rory. All his compositions were published by Strange Music, his own company, thus enabling him to retain both artistic freedom and the copyright on his music.

Once the album had been cut, Gerry went home to Belfast. But another phone call brought him back. Rory asked him to accompany him on his tour. Donal became the group's tour manager. The band's adventure began in Paris, in a televised concert at the Olympia: Gerry's first experience of such a show.

That year, 1971, Rory began a gruelling, concert-after-concert world tour. Rory, Gerry and Wilgar hit the road, destination Europe and the United States of America.

*Donal Gallagher's business card following the*
*creation of 'Strange Music', Rory's music company*

# BILZEN

Father Maurice Paul closed the door of the presbytery next to Bilzen Chapel. Night fell on the tiny Flemish hamlet wedged between the borders of Germany, the Netherlands and French-speaking Belgium. The priest strode purposefully towards one of the cafés on the market place. He stepped in the door, moved towards the bar and ordered a beer. The bartender told him that the others were waiting for him in the back room. There were about twenty of them, and they all welcomed the newcomer.

The priest shook hands and smiled, fixing his glasses as he un-did the jacket that held in his ample midriff. He sat down and lis-tened attentively to the remarks made by the chairman of the group, Jan Caugh, a small, grey-haired man. 'The Rory Gallagher contract has been signed,' he said. 'We're just waiting for the group Family.'

The Bilzen Jazz Festival was a family affair, organised by a com-mittee of twenty-five people. The entire village got involved for the bank holiday weekend of 15 August, with everyone attending the musical Mass on Sunday morning, celebrated by Father Maurice

Paul, with the participation of the jazzmen. The first festival had taken place in 1965, and from 1967 the line-up had got bigger and bigger. In 1968, rock-and-blues artists such as Procol Harum, the Small Faces, the Pretty Things and Alexis Korner rubbed shoulders with jazz greats Dizzie Gillespie, Archie Shepp, Sonny Rollins and Gato Barbieri. In less than a decade, the crowd had grown from 6,000 festival-goers in 1968 to 50,000 in 1975. In 1971, the festival ran into a number of problems linked to this swell in numbers, instigated by a few left-wing activists from France in an attempt to destabilise the festival. Such upheavals were nothing new at that time, especially when a uniformed, truncheoned police presence became obvious. On stage, however, there was an impressive line-up: the Faces, John McLaughlin and Colosseum,

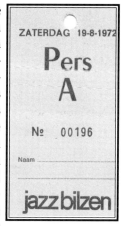

ZATERDAG 19-8-1972

**Pers
A**

№ 00196

Naam

**jazzbilzen**

*Backstage press pass from 1972 given to the journalists attending the Bilzen festival*

with their new singer, Chris Farlowe, who was a childhood friend of Mick Jagger's and who was blessed with a powerful voice. Family tried out their new bass player, John Wetton, and the young folk singer Al Stewart dazzled everybody. The Reverend Gary Davis, an old, blind, black bluesman and near-mythical Piemont-blues figure, gave an incredible lesson in modesty by virtue of his great humility, allied with immense talent. Jean Luc Ponty also took part, accompanied by German pianist Joachim Khun.

Rory Gallagher and his new group made a strong impact on the festival-goers and were warmly received. The rapport between Rory and his audience was electric, and the crowd instantly took Gerry McAvoy and Wilgar Campbell to their hearts. From that moment on, Belgium came to be a favourite stopover point for the band. Backstage, Noeghan, with his Nagra over his shoulder, met Rory for an interview.

On the muddy path that led to Rory's caravan, he had crossed Pete Brown and Graham Bond making their way towards the stage, followed by Roland from Blues Workshop, looking relaxed and holding the hand of his partner, Catherine. She was an amateur photographer, and her camera was slung over her shoulder, but she was also a much sought-after model, a woman of beauty, simplicity, wit, intelligence and sensitivity. With a long Indian skirt and loose black hair, she was radiantly stunning. Noeghan looked at her, but she

*Rory at Bilzen*

didn't see him. As of yet, they didn't know each other. In fact, Roland didn't know Rory, who didn't know Noeghan, who didn't know Roland – at least for the time being.

Always extremely accommodating, Rory gave Noeghan a short interview. He introduced Gerry and Wilgar, said nothing about the reasons behind recent changes, and confided, 'I could live without recording, but I couldn't live without playing live.' During the interview, Larry Coryell was on stage, accompanied by John Marshall and John Battington. When the interview ended, Rory too joined the audience, where he was spotted by Coryell, who invited him on stage.

As Tom O'Driscoll brought over his Stratocaster, Rory's fingers were itching to play, and the ensuing live jam was inevitable. Together, Larry and Rory set the audience on fire with their fusion of jazz and blues-rock.

*Bilzen, from left to right: Larry Coryell, John Marshall, John Battington, Rory*

## DEUCE

*Deuce*, the second album from the Rory–Gerry–Wilgar trio, was recorded at Tangerine Studios in London with sound engineer Robin Sylvester. The album was symbolic of Rory's never-ending quest, his journey into the heart of a musical vision that was undoubtedly his own, only then to evolve along very different paths, some of which were disconcerting for purists. His trademark was stamped on all the tracks of the album: 'Used to Be', with its aggressive vocals and cutting guitar, for instance, and the explosive 'In Your Town', a rock classic later to be exploited by Thin Lizzy's 'Jailbreak'. All Rory's energy and power are carried by the raw, vivacious notes of his

*Rory in Liège*

guitar. 'Should've Learned My Lesson' is classic, weighty blues. 'Out of My Mind' is a real gem, with magical acoustic guitar and voice. In a more traditional folk style, 'Don't Know Where I'm Going' combines acoustic guitar and harmonica with the discreet presence of Gerry and Wilgar. The more intimate tracks include 'I'm Not Awake Yet', with moving vocals, gripping rhythm and versatile guitar. 'Maybe I Will', and 'Whole Lot of People' are catchy rock tracks with amazing slide guitar. In 'There's a Light', Rory moves around a traditional jazz framework, whereas on 'Crest of a Wave', the slide guitar again dazzles, rises and crashes against a frenetic rhythm. 'Persuasion', a mid-tempo Celtic track, with Rory's wonderful voice scatting with his guitar, is a bonus track. *Deuce* captures all of Rory's potential.

# THE TRAIN

Like the low rumbling of a runaway train, the hellish, metallic fury of a throbbing beat and staccato rattling, the track began with the magic of John Mayall on harmonica. A voice-over announced the groups, starting with Rory Gallagher, as 'Going to My Home Town' blasted out in breathtaking style.

The Belgian radio engineers were surprisingly efficient, putting their programmes together without cutting the reels, then making copies straight onto tape. This was an art in itself. They would find the required sentence from an interview, or the intro to a song, and in a flash, the finished product would be ready. The soundbite for Pop Circus had already been recorded, and was about to be played on air. The concert was to take place in Liège in the spring of 1972, the line-up bringing together a number of Belgian groups – Assagai, Vinegar Joe and some other artists in vogue at the time – and Rory Gallagher. The Rory Gallagher Band was everywhere. Despite the fact that *Deuce* had barely been released, a live album had already been planned and recorded on their recent European tour. It was an explosive album, of which they had only one copy in their possession: an unmarked vinyl in an unsealed sleeve. The music spoke for itself, vibrant and dazzling, packed with feeling, energy, passion and emotion. For some, it was a revelation. This Irish guy who trailed his old Fender guitar across all the stages of Europe, and later the world, intrigued Noeghan. During their first encounters, he felt no jolt nor shock, more a transfer of emotion. Drop by drop, little by little, the music poured into him like *aqua vitae*. It was already appar-

*Station platform: Gerry McAvoy, Rory, Wilgar Campbell, X, and Claude Delacroix*

*In the train, from left to right, Gerry McAvoy, Rory and X*

ent to him just how drawn to this music he was, and whatever restraint or shyness he felt only led him to a deeper understanding of it, whereby, without any rush, he seized it, absorbed it, and lived it. This music was his music, the mother of all music, which from that moment on was to make her mark upon him and become vital to him. Unbeknown to him, his initiation was complete.

Enthusiastic, indeed flustered, Noeghan brought up the subject of the live album and the concert, with his programme producer, Claude Delacroix, presenting him with an idea: organising a train to leave Brussels, taking all the concert-goers, along with the groups and other musicians, to Liège. The 'Formula J' train was on the tracks. In the wee small hours of the morning, there was a very curious atmosphere in the Brussels railway station. Hundreds of long-haired youths in jeans and denim jackets took the dilapidated carriages of the train by storm. Fans were to travel with the artists they loved, hopping from one carriage to another, everyone rubbing shoulders with each other. Even the Belgian conductors were polite!

In Liège, Elkie Brooks from Vinegar Joe was on stage, looking divine with her long hair, split skirt and high heels. Another group member, quite a dandy, and looking as if he had been poured into his black leather trousers, was rising young star Robert Palmer – not forgetting the lead guitarist and self-professed Dadaist Peter Cage.

Rory, Gerry and Wilgar set the place alight. The concert lasted an uncompromising three hours. The conquered crowd was overwhelmed, the victory hard-hitting and fast-paced, with track after track linked by cries and applause: 'Messing with Your Kid', 'In Your Town', 'I Could've Had Religion', 'Laundromat'.

When Rory picked up his acoustic guitar, an almost religious silence reigned. Alone on stage, his folk and country songs transported the thousands of fans to a higher plane. The crowd screamed for joy as he picked up the mandolin. The chords rang out as, with a resounding voice, he launched into 'Going to My Home Town'. The audience clapped their hands, stamped their feet, beat out the rhythm and hammered the ground. Gerry and Wilgar reappeared. Gerry's eyes were glued to Rory, as he raised his hands to the beat. Wilgar slipped in behind his kit and picked up the tempo. It all came together like a roller-coaster ride. The climax of the set was 'Bullfrog Blues', where Rory, after long, intricate flights of solo guitar, put his fellow musicians in the spotlight. Gerry gave a fabulous bass solo, after which Wilgar kicked into a thunderous exhibition of drumming. The crowd was delighted, and Rory was content.

Backstage, there were improvised dressing-rooms. Sitting down on a chair, Rory caught his breath, his face dripping with sweat, and his guitar leaning nearby.

He took another towel from his bag, rubbed his face with it and wrapped it around his neck. Gerry handed him a change of trousers while Wilgar, bare-chested, drank from a bottle of water. Rory caught sight of Noeghan, and beckoned him over. Once again, Rory was available for an interview, in which he swapped impressions of the concert, gave details about the *Live in Europe* album, and announced a planned tour in the States.

Noeghan, seduced, decided that night in his heart of hearts that he would live this experience first-hand. He felt the need to discover

*Liège: Wilgar Campbell (drums), Gerry McAvoy (bass) view from behind, Rory*

all aspects of this music, which, in its inspiration, vitality, vigour, violence and emotion, without any compromise or artifice, was the very image of its creator.

The public was not mistaken. Despite being totally independent of the Top Ten system and rarely given radio airtime, Rory had a huge following. In their thousands they attended his concerts, in their thousands they bought his albums, with *Live in Europe* (including the tracks 'Messin' with the Kid', 'Laundromat', 'I Could've Had Religion', 'Pistol-slapper Blues', 'Going to My Home Town', 'In Your Town', 'What in the World', 'Hoochoo Man' and 'Bullfrog Blues') going platinum, in their thousands they voted for Rory Gallagher in *Melody Maker*'s Pop Poll, making him its 'Best Musician of 1972'. To this public accolade must be added those of his fellow musicians and heroes. Muddy Waters, passing through London for a recording session, invited Rory to sit in with him.

## MUDDY WATERS

McKinley Morganfield, or Muddy Waters, was one of Rory's heroes, his spiritual father. This was the same Muddy Waters – born 4 April 1915 in Mississippi, died 30 April 1983 in Chicago – who asked Rory to participate in recording *London Sessions*. Rory felt greatly honoured. That session followed one under the Chess label, with Howlin' Wolf. The idea was to put the blues fathers in a studio, along with their usual musicians and the white musicians of the British blues who were responsible for the recent revival of the genre. Charlie Watts, Bill Wyman, Eric Clapton, Ian Stewart and Stevie Winwood had all participated in the Howlin' Wolf session. For the Muddy Waters recording, they recruited Rory Gallagher, Mitch Mitchell, Georgie Fame, Rick Gretch, masters of the Carey Bell Harrington harmonica, and Sam Hawthorne, to complement Rory's guitar. For Rory, this was a great honour, and a real pleasure. Muddy and Rory got along very well, having the same style and way of doing things, their personalities being very similar. Both were hard-working, determined, indeed painstaking in their work, with a respect for others. Both were perfect gentlemen. Rory cherished very fond memories of that recording session. 'Muddy himself played the guitar,' he recalled, 'and with him were Chicago blues-type musicians. It was a rather mixed session, with both European and American musicians. With Muddy Waters, everything is cool. He knows what he wants and where he wants to go. He has his tracks written down in a list ... The session lasted four nights.'

Recording started in December 1971 at London's IBC Studios. The links between the musicians were amazing. Mitch Mitchell (Hendrix's drummer) and Georgie Fame were present, along with Stevie Winwood, who had taken part in the Electric Ladybird session with Hendrix and Mitchell and had also been a member of Blind Faith along with Rick Gretch. Rory's first tour of the United States was with Blind Faith, and it was on that very tour that he met Muddy Waters, and perhaps Hendrix. The icing on the cake was the fact that the album was mixed at the Electric Ladybird Studios, which had been set up by Hendrix in New York.

Gerry remembers that some time later, during a tour of the United States, the group went to a Muddy Waters concert in New York. Among those at the concert was Steve Marriott, whose group Humble Pie was very much in vogue. Muddy Waters had been told that they were there, and mentioned their names. At the end of a song, Waters called out for 'Rory Marriott' to join him on stage. At that, they both stepped forward and joined him – an unforgettable moment.

## ORESTE BLUES

It was 1944. Events in Eastern Europe were causing a massive influx of refugees, mainly from the Ukraine. Traumatised populations were plunged into the horror of war, hatred and executions, and the Nazis' massive deportations to labour camps. At the end of the war, many could not bear to go home, especially once the Soviet influence began to manifest itself. France decided to allow its refugees to stay, for it needed strong arms to help post-war reconstruction.

The humanitarian convoy, which arrived in Bordeaux, spilled its contents – a tide of immigrants – onto the platform, in a strange silence broken only by the incomprehensible female voice of the loudspeaker. Women with little white hats marked with red crosses welcomed the lost and tired travellers. The end of a journey? The end of a nightmare?

In September 1945 people with exhausted, haggard faces, torn clothes and ragged children, too tired to cry, filled the station with their bits and pieces, in boxes and bags. Freedom. Barbara, with her round belly, supported her friend Katarina, who herself was seven months pregnant. In an endless queue, they went through the registration formalities, which were rather basic, as not many of them spoke French. They were directed to the camp, where accommodation had already been stretched to 3,500 refugees. It was there, in a tent, that Katarina gave birth to a son, on 1 November. His name was Oreste, which in English became 'Richard'. Barbara, who herself became 'Ahafia' thanks to the efforts of an overworked Polish–German translator, gave birth in December to another baby boy, called Stephen. Life went on. During the months that followed, the refugees were dispersed across France. The mothers of Stephen and Richard were sent to Roubaix in the north of France, where they settled in an old textile factory, on Rue du Nouveau Monde – New World Street! They had dreamed of settling in America. In Roubaix they were stranded in a huge, cold, empty space with no belongings; fruit and vegetable boxes served as furniture and as divisions between the areas in which the families tried to maintain some semblance of intimacy. To heat milk for Stephen and Richard, there was one saucepan, shared by five or six families. But jobs appeared quickly, and the boys' mothers found themselves positions as factory workers. They had barely enough clothes, never mind shoes, and walked barefoot along the frozen pavement.

Months and years went by; conditions improved. They earned almost-decent salaries, and the families moved into houses of their own. The women became integrated, and the children grew up and attended school. Community life was very strong, centred on the church. People helped each other out and kept in touch with others who had found asylum. They gathered for family meals, which always ended with music and dancing. Richard had been playing banjo and guitar since the age of ten, playing in a local orchestra. His friend Stephen went along too, but not for long. Destiny was soon to separate them, for Richard's mother left and joined other friends in Britain who were also refugees. She remarried. Richard left Roubaix to go with his mother and stepfather to England. Years went by, and the two mothers continued to keep in touch, but the children didn't.

Stephen and Noeghan, who were from the same neighbourhood, shared the same group of friends and hung out together. One day, Stephen, who knew nothing about rock music, told Noeghan that his mother had received news about one of his childhood friends. Apparently, this person had toured America with a well-known group and recorded something. On the cover of the recording there was a doll's house, with his friend sitting in a bath. Stephen asked Noeghan if he knew of any album like that. Noeghan, in shock, said nothing. He got up and went over to his pile of records. He picked up the black cover of the Family album *Music in a Doll's House* and handed it to Stephen, who looked at the figure sitting in the bathtub and exclaimed, 'That's him! Richard, my mate Richard! That's Rick, Rick Gretch!'

*Rory during TV recording in the RTB studios*

## BAND OF GYPSIES

'I don't want to go! I don't want to go! I don't want to!' Wilgar Campbell was in a state, couldn't cope any more, and broke down in tears. He was of a very nervous temperament and could not stand flying. It made him ill. But that June morning, the group was in Geneva. The concert the previous evening had gone according to plan, but after a hard night, Wilgar cracked. He couldn't continue the tour; he couldn't cope with the flights. Wilgar laid down his drumsticks and left the group, although later he played with a number of other bands. At that time, Gerry was sharing a flat in London with a drummer called Rod de Ath, a Welshman who had played with Killing Floor. Gerry called him immediately and asked whether he could help them out. That evening, he played with them in Limerick, and joined the group. Rory, Gerry and Rod toured together for three months, also recording a television programme for the BBC. Indeed, according to the BBC, Rory was their most recorded musician at that time. Rory also found himself a pianist, Lou Martin, an Irishman who had been part of the same group as Rod. Rory had seen their group several times in concert. Lou was an excellent blues player, and they invited him to accompany them on their tour of Italy. The trio became a quartet, like a band of gypsies, according to Gerry: a bohemian group who played from town to town. They would arrive with their instruments, play, stay the night, and leave the next day. That lasted twenty years – and thousands upon thousands of concerts.

# BLUEPRINT

The band started work on the album *Blueprint*, recorded in London's Marquee Studios with Polydor. The keyboards are omnipresent from the very first track and are well and truly part of the album, not just an added extra. Lou Martin's touch in 'Daughter of the Everglades' confers magnificent solemnity upon this somewhat nostalgic composition. Their cover of 'Banker's Blues', a Big Bill Bronzy classic, is given a 'piano' facelift in Chicago-blues style, fitting in perfectly with Rory's guitar. The notes blend with an ease that reveals, by their cohesion, true complicity, indeed communion, between the musicians – which continues throughout the album. Other classics are 'Hands Off' and 'Race the Breeze', whereas a track such as 'The Seventh Son of the Seventh Son' is emblematic of a very different musical approach. On this track, Rory reveals a sensitivity that may surprise some of his fans. 'Unmilitary Two-step' is an instrumental track, played solely on acoustic guitar, resembling a soundtrack to a 1920s silent film.

A strange sigh envelops the lapsteel guitar of 'If I Had a Reason', emphasising Rory's fondness for country music. In any case, this was a key album. The remastered CD has two bonus tracks, 'Stompin' Ground' (Rory was very pleased to arrive home in Cork after touring) and 'Treat Her Right' (he had always enjoyed performing this Roy Head favourite with the Fontana Showband).

# THE RORY FORMULA

Lieve was a tiny, plump woman, but a fighter, and a true professional. As press agent with Polydor in Belgium, she was wickedly efficient and fought tooth-and-nail for her artists. Chas Chandler, Slade, Neil Sedaka, James Brown, Elie Greenwich, Freddie King and many others – including Rory Gallagher – were all very grateful to her. Following his arrival in Belgium for a series of concerts for a TV channel, Lieve played a key role. She took care of 'her' artist, managed the schedule, made the hotel arrangements along with the promoters, booked restaurants and organised advertising. She did her utmost for her protégés and was, in a word, indispensable. Rory, like the others, realised this, and trusted her. Noeghan held Lieve in very high esteem, and his working relationship with this energetic Flemish woman, who left nothing to chance, quickly turned into a mutual friendship, the close rapport between Chas Chandler, Slade and Noeghan strengthening this link. In March 1973, Rory was expected in Belgium for a series of concerts organised by one of the country's largest promoters, Paul Ambach. Noeghan wanted to dedicate an entire radio programme to Rory, because on the Friday, the day of Rory's arrival in Belgium, the *Formula J* programme was to be broadcast live and in public from the National Book Show *(Salon du Livre)*. The programme's presenter, Claude Delacroix, immediately warmed to the idea of having Rory live on Belgian national radio. The only person who was not informed of this was Rory himself, the star of the show!

Lieve promised to help. She called London and spoke to her Polydor colleague Clive Wood, who told her that it would be up to Rory to decide whether to appear on the show. Lieve gave Noeghan the arrival time of his flight at Zaventem Airport in Brussels. Rory arrived that morning with Gerry, Lou and Rod, dressed in a leather jacket and woolly scarf, carrying a small holdall. He headed towards Lieve and kissed her, and the group made their way to the exit, where Noeghan was waiting for them. Lieve grabbed Rory, while beckoning Noeghan over. Rory greeted him with a nod of his head as Lieve explained their schedule. 'You're free all day until the concert, the radio programme would be late afternoon,' she said. Evasively, Rory agreed in principle, but no meeting was arranged. Rory and his musicians climbed into their limousine and set off for their hotel, near the main square in the centre of Brussels.

*Zaventem: Jean-Noël Coghe, Lieve, Rory*

'Go and meet up with him at the hotel this afternoon,' Lieve had hissed as she closed the door of the limousine. 'I'll try and get it sorted out!'

Noeghan got into his car and drove to Brussels, where he was staying with friends, the parents of his godson. John Valcke played bass with the group Wallace Collection, who were very popular at that time. After their hit 'Daydream', they wrote the soundtrack for the film *La Maison*, with Michel Simon. Claudia, herself a press agent and close friend of Lieve, was also the manager of a clothes shop. She bought some of her stock from a young fashion designer in London, whom she met shortly afterwards when he played, still in relative anonymity, in Brussels with his group. Noeghan, who was with her, was actually wearing one of the jackets the guy had designed and made. The designer was Freddie Mercury, who later hooked up, musically, with Brian May, and Queen was born.

Noeghan, not completely certain of Rory's participation, tentatively planned the broadcast nonetheless; the programme was to include a brief outline of Rory's life, his albums and the recording session with Muddy Waters. Meanwhile, Claude Delacroix scheduled a back-up broadcast, just in case! Then they waited. Noeghan went to visit Claudia, in an attempt to calm his nerves, at her shop in the Galerie Agora, right beside the main square – and Rory's hotel. Claudia devoured a sandwich, but Noeghan couldn't swallow a bite. He fidgeted impatiently while Claudia teased him.

'Look, there's your Rory,' she giggled, gulping back her last bite of sandwich.

'You think you're so funny,' Noeghan replied dryly.

With these very words, however, the door opened and Rory stepped into the shop. Alone, anonymous, he had gone for a lunch-time stroll, and by pure chance had happened upon that very shop. Seeing Noeghan, he smiled and moved towards him, uttered a few words and examined the clothes: lizard-skin jackets, platform boots, tie-dyed T-shirts, lamé trousers. These were eccentric clothes screaming bad taste, the very latest fashion, which Rory would never have worn, diametrically opposed as it was to his personality, contradicting his simplicity. Yet he came into the shop! Suddenly, looking Noeghan in the eyes, not at all surprised to have come across him by sheer luck, he said, 'It's cool about the programme. I'll come back here around four.' And as quickly as he had come, he left.

Rory arrived on time, alone. Noeghan showed him to the car. The broadcast was to take place at the Martini Centre, which housed the National Book Show. The studio was right in the heart of the centre, with the general public gathering on the other side of its glass screens. Rory sat down in front of the microphone and smiled as he listened to the programme's signature tune, by Led Zeppelin. Led Zeppelin had still been called the New Yardbirds when they played with Taste. The red light came on, and Delacroix announced their special guest. The telephone rang, and questions from the listeners poured in. Rory, looking relaxed, felt right at home. *Formula J* gave him two hours of airtime. At the end of the programme, Rory, touched and surprised, participated graciously in an impromptu autograph session. It was nearly seven when they left the show. Noeghan drove Rory back to the city centre. On getting out of the car, Rory suggested that they go and get something to eat. Noeghan hesitated, thinking that Rory owed him nothing at all, but Rory urged him on, saying that it would be a pleasure for him. Noeghan accepted, and the two men wandered down the Rue des Bouchers, just behind the Grand Place, where six years previously Noeghan had taken Jimi Hendrix to eat. They ate in small restaurant just opposite the Toone puppet theatre. Rory ordered soup and drank a little beer, or maybe it was red wine. Noeghan could hardly remember which: he was a little overawed. Here they were, the pair of them – they didn't know each other, yet they were sitting down to dinner like two old buddies. The silence was as weighty as the conversation. For almost two hours they talked about everything and nothing: music, the south of France, Jimi Hendrix. They talked about what they liked, their lives, their friends. At the end of the simple meal, Rory asked for the bill, refusing Noeghan's offer to pay half. 'Are you coming to the concert tonight?' Rory asked. Noeghan replied that of course he was. 'Would you mind driving us there?' Noeghan, delighted but amazed, accepted. In the hotel foyer, they bumped into Tom O'Driscoll, who was already leaving for Theatre 140. Lou, Gerry and Rod were ready, waiting with their promoter, Paul Ambach. The same Paul Ambach had worked with the Rolling Stones, Led Zeppelin, Frank Sinatra and many others in Belgium. He was also known as Boogie Boy and he had played with BB King. Rory greeted him, and explained that Noeghan was going to drive them to the venue. Paul agreed wholeheartedly to this plan, and indeed suggested that Noeghan be their guide for the duration of their three-day stay.

Theatre 140 was packed. It was a mythical venue, where every concert metamorphosed into an event. With its small capacity – it held no more that 500 people – Theatre 140 was always packed to the

*Rory, Theatre 140*

71

rafters, with the audience on benches, even on the stage. All this generated a kind of magic that transcended the show itself. Pink Floyd, Velvet Underground the Family, Frank Zappa jamming with Ten Years After, Queen, and many more had rocked Theatre 140, and still haunt its boards, along with the memories of those who were privileged enough to have lived through such rare, moments. Rory Gallagher became part of the myth. It was his first visit to Belgium with his new musicians: Gerry on bass, and reinforcements Rod de Ath, on drums, and Lou Martin, on keyboards. Lou made an important contribution to the sound and feel of the group. At the piano or organ, he accentuated and elaborated upon the riffs and effects of Rory's guitar, without going over the top. He blended excellently with the powerful drum and bass. The songs written and scored for the former Rory Gallagher trio benefited immensely from the presence of the keyboards – an added extra which served to make the music even more memorable.

The crowd in Theatre 140 that gave Rory a standing ovation were not mistaken. With Rory, everything was intense. After the concert, a dinner had been organised in the hotel restaurant. The musicians sat around the table in silence. Waiting to order, Lou flicked through a book, Gerry stared at a candle flame, Rod beat a rhythm with his

*[From left to right] Rod de Ath, Lou Martin, Gerry McAvoy, Rory*

fork, and Rory, at the end of the table, was deep in thought. Each one appeared to be coming around after the intensity of the previous hours, and preparing for those ahead. Every moment of the day, every event, no matter how small, was part of the next concert. Everything stretched out towards them and came together at that vital moment, when the bright lights flooded the stage and Rory ran on to greet the public who were calling for him, reaching out their arms to him. He always went to them, shaking their hands. There was no crowd-control, no muscular arms to prevent or forbid such contact. With Rory there was a great energy to transform or transport. There was no aggression. There was fire but no provocation, fighting spirit but no brutality.

The next concert, in Courtrai, a Flemish town on the French border, and on the linguistic border of French-speaking Belgium, was rather symbolic. Crowds from the city of Lille in the north of France came and mixed not only with their Flemish neighbours but also with those from French-speaking Belgium. Once again, through the magic of his music Rory brought together three deeply divided communities.

For those three days, Noeghan stuck to the Rory Gallagher Band. A friendship was being forged.

# LIVERPOOL

Under a burning sun, the whole town was out on the streets. Men, women and children lined the pavements as tension filled the air. The police were out in force and on the alert, ready to intervene along with other security forces, who had also been mobilised for the event. For the last few months, the situation across the Irish Sea had been worrying, with fatal bomb attacks in Belfast. Many innocent lives had been lost, victims of extremists on both sides of the community. Liverpool itself on this hot, sunny day was practically on the verge of war. It was 12 July, the commemoration of William of Orange's Protestant victory in 1690 over the Catholic King James II. The battle was celebrated each year with an Orange Order march through the city. It was out with flags, banners, slogans, beer, animosity and hatred. People thronged the route of the march in their thousands to see them walk, to shout with them, to boo at yesterday's enemy, perhaps today's neighbour. There were several hundred of them marching. Some of them, faces expressionless, walked in step, military-style. Others, more worked up, struck up warlike, 'kick-the-pope' songs. The men were drunk and aggressive, and were quickly surrounded by mounted police officers, who moved in to quell them without warning, truncheons raised, trying to contain the marchers, and attempting at all costs to prevent them leaving the body of the parade. In Liverpool, with its social deprivation, there was a large Irish population, and during such troubled times there was always the threat of bomb attacks.

Mingling with the crowd, Noeghan heard military-style music in the distance, the sound of footsteps thundering along the road, and voices raised in a swelling din of shouts, songs and horses' hooves. The crowd pushed forward to catch a glimpse. A flag-bearer was making his way along the middle of the road in more of a stagger than a march, his face haggard and dripping with sweat, eyes bulging. Noeghan sensed a deep feeling of unease as the hand he held squeezed his tight, as if hanging on for dear life, desperately trying to conquer her almost tangible fear. The hand was that of Lesley-Ann, who for three days had been Noeghan's guide in Liverpool, showing him the sites, from the Cavern to Penny Lane. She was certainly Irish, perhaps even Catholic! It mattered little. She had had enough of such a permanent state of war, the constant conflict, the killing, the slaughter, all of which affected her greatly.

During these troubled times, Rory continued to play in Northern Ireland, as he had done regularly since 1966. With his background, he was very aware of the issues at stake. In Cork, he had set up Taste with Eric Kitteringham and Norman Damery, both natives of Cork, and both Protestant. The group established a certain notoriety for itself in Northern Ireland by playing in Belfast to both sides of the community. With the second Taste line-up, this approach was even more evident as John Wilson and Richard McCracken were both Belfast Protestants.

In Belfast, the pubs had grills on their windows, there were body-searches in the streets, and certain areas of strategic importance remained under spotlight all night. The city echoed with the sirens of ambulances and the noise of the police, British army patrols, the Royal Irish Regiment and the omnipresent helicopters. On the walls of the Nationalist neighbourhoods were etched slogans in support of the IRA. In the Unionist districts the graffiti supported the army. Some 'Prods' also supported the Ulster Volunteer Force, the Ulster Freedom Fighters and the Ulster Defence Association. Bombings were carried out by both sides. People were tired of counting the dead and injured: too much innocent blood had been spilled. But the inhabitants of Northern Ireland shared with the rest of Ireland whiskey, Guinness and even the 'Ulster fry'. They also shared their violence. The 'Red Hand' of Ulster was particularly symbolic. History had it that the first person to touch the soil of Ulster would be its king. A group of lords were fighting their way towards its shoreline, each set on conquering and ruling the area. One of them, called O'Neill, was so driven that, on nearing the coast, he took his sword and cut off his hand, throwing it onto the beach. The Red Hand has since become the symbol of the loyalists, an ancestral reminder of bloodshed.

Ireland is primarily a country of individualism and rebellion. The laws of the land were forged according to the Brehon laws, which strengthened existing customs, with respect for regional particularities and differences. These rules were unchallenged until the Norman invasion. Caesar never managed to conquer Ireland and impose Roman rule there. But Norman law, derived from Roman law, was incompatible with the Brehon system, and this sowed the seeds of conflict and resistance. What a loss. France profited from the Irish, who were defeated at Kinsale, County Cork, fled and lent their services to the French army. They enrolled in their thousands, and were nicknamed the Wild Geese. It was thanks to one of these regiments that the French were victorious at the Battle of Fontenoy in 1745.

Fifty-three years later, after a French marine disaster in which the fleet got lost in the fog, a group of French officers led by Jean-Joseph Humbert went to the help of the Irish. A thousand French soldiers landed in Ireland and defeated 6,000 English at Castlebar. But on the road to Dublin, faced with 36,000 troops, they were defeated, at Ballinamuck.


So Rory continued to play in Northern Ireland. Taste had shown that music could cut across the divide, no matter how deep this was. Their fans were young people, Nationalists and Unionists whose hearts beat to the same rhythm, who would never have got together in the same venue had it not been for their shared passion for this group. Taste was a perfect example for them: two Protestants from Belfast, and a Catholic from Cork. They worked together and made music together, proving that you could be from a different religion yet live the same passion. What a lesson for such hardened kids.

Rory brought the two sections of the community together, for in his concerts everyone mixed together, and the crowd was practically indistinguishable, bar their school scarves that served to differentiate them. These were a distinctive symbol of 'belonging', even in concerts in the Ulster Hall in Belfast. Other than that, there was no telling them apart. 'They shared the same Taste,' said Donal. Rory brought them together with his music, and indeed was alone in achieving this. Rory played in Belfast several times in the early 1970s, during the most dangerous years of the Troubles. The other musicians, including Van Morrison, had left, only to come back later.

Rory played again in the Ulster Hall, on Bedford Street, which was also known as 'Bomb Alley' because of its position in a busy shopping street, an ideal target. It was a concert hall and a church, the favourite haunt of the Reverend Ian Paisley, who preached there every week. For years, the hall was the largest venue in Belfast city, and was only ever full for Paisley or Rory. At the time of Taste, there were no decent dressing-rooms for the musicians. Although there was a room set aside for such purposes, it was always padlocked, reserved for Paisley. One evening Taste threatened not to play unless they were allowed into the dressing-room. The hall was full, and rather than risk a riot, Rory was allowed into the holy of holies.

The young people who made up Rory's fan base were part of a generation who today are striving towards peace. They were united at his concerts, brought together by music, the true standard of peace. In 1998, John Hume and David Trimble were awarded the Nobel Peace Prize for their part in the peace process. Rory was among those who brought about such an evolution, the birth of a peace movement. His role in this movement was significant and should not be ignored.

*Rory,*
*Liège 1976*

# GUITAR

Rory only felt at ease on stage. Tour followed tour at an infernal rate, and Rory's band travelled back and forth across Europe, Scandinavia and the United States. He did more than 200 concerts a year, and spent roughly three hours on stage per concert, with his faithful companion pressed against his side. After thousands of gigs, however, his guitar rather capriciously began to cause him a few problems. Rory could not tune it properly, and a closer examination revealed that the neck of the Stratocaster was warped and out of shape – the neck which Leo Fender had invented in the 1940s, in his workshop on the west coast of the United States. Rory was alarmed, and the guitar was dismantled, the neck sent to Fender in America for repair. This proved to be impossible, and the faulty neck was sent back to him, with a replacement part that Rory then fixed onto his guitar. The warped neck sat on a windowsill in Rory's flat for months. One day he happened to pick it up, only to discover that it had straightened out and was as good as new. Rory put it back on his guitar and tuned it, and the tour went ahead as planned, the Stratocaster reunited with its original neck.

The change in shape of the neck of the guitar was due to a buildup of moisture. On stage, Rory gave his all, perspiring profusely. This perspiration then soaked into his guitar, causing it to warp. The wood of the neck reacted violently to the excess moisture, and bent, only later drying out and bending back to its original shape. At the same time, the paint on the body of the guitar was peeling off. Some people thought that Rory intentionally created such an 'ageing', the flaking paint giving his guitar a worn, threadbare look. Actually, once more it was Rory's perspiration that caused the paint to peel. He also had a very rare blood group with a high acid content. The paint, when in contact with the acidity carried by his perspiration, disintegrated and peeled away. The wood was stripped. So, with his own sweat and blood, Rory created a very special guitar.

Rory also made a few modifications, especially to the guitar's electronics. He liked musical effects; although he wasn't a great fan of the wah-wah pedal, he still wanted to be able to alter the guitar's sound and change its tone or volume with his little finger. He changed the controls on his guitar and operated them at will to obtain the sound he desired, or to give it shape. Rory made his Stratocaster into a unique model, which today is venerated like some sort of religious relic. Since his death, it lies in its original case, locked away in a strongbox in a bank, awaiting the day when it will be on show in a museum. While it was at Donal's home, following its return from Fender, Donal opened up the case and looked at it, with a hint of emotion and sadness. Turning to Noeghan, who had lent over to look, Rory said, 'It'll never be played again', as he shivered and swallowed back his tears. Donal saw his emotion. 'Here,' he said to the Stratocaster, 'look, Noeghan's back.' He lifted the guitar delicately and placed it in Noeghan's arms, who gently held it as one would a dear friend after a long, cruel absence. He was overcome by the gesture.

*Rory's stratocaster, on stage, waiting for the concert*

There are now copies of this unique model. Fender made a limited-edition Rory Gallagher Stratocaster, an exact replica of his guitar. This model had already sold out prior to its introduction at a Frankfurt trade fair in 2000. Donal took the original to Fender in California, where they took it apart, studied it closely and produced a perfect copy, right down to the ageing paint, tiny scratches and scrapes. Master craftsman John English, who carried out the work, did so with respect, even devotion. He had lived in Belgium in the early 1970s and had gone to several of Rory's concerts. This reassured Donal. 'He's family,' he said.

# TATTOO

Nineteen seventy-three was a prolific year for Rory's band. Rory and his musicians were in the Polydor studios, recording *Tattoo*. It was packed with diverse tracks and genres, all stamped with Rory's signature. Some of them, such as 'Tattoo'd Lady', which comes alive to a burst of accordion, were to become classics and were played on stage for years afterwards. The complicity between the guitar and Lou's keyboards is undeniable. 'Cradle Rock' was another splendid rock classic, which would set a concert on fire. It was a powerful track, scattered with moments that would run down into silence before exploding once again into a pulsating rhythm and wonderful bass-line. The organ sounds and snippets of harmonica urge the guitar on to ever-greater delirium. 'Cradle Rock' is a serious rock track. Rory used a Silverstone guitar in his recording, which he had purchased for fifteen dollars. '20:20 Vision' is a finely polished acoustic track, with a guitar–piano exchange in the country-blues style. 'Livin' Like a Trucker' lives up to its title, whereas 'They Don't Make Them Like You Any More' is more chiselled, as is the delicate 'Sleep on a Clothes Line'. The Dobro debut, a genre in which Rory excelled, made its entrance in 'Who's That Coming', to be overtaken by vigorous electric and slide guitar. Piano and harmonica blend in. With his Silverstone guitar, a Dan Electro, Rory also recorded 'A Million Miles Away', a superb, poignant track that dies away with a hint of saxophone. The album finishes with 'Admit It'. The CD, which was remastered by Tony Arnold, features two bonus tracks: 'Tucson Arizona', a country track from Link Wray, and 'Just a Little Bit'. 'This track,' says Donal, 'gives an insight into the affinity and good humour that existed between Rory and his sidemen.'

# JERRY LEE LEWIS

'The Killer' was in London, the city which had hunted him down in the 1960s, when Jerry Lee Lewis had married his fourteen-year-old cousin. Lewis was now in London to record a double album, bringing together a dazzling array of musicians, hitherto never seen together, all united for the maddest of rock stars. Taking part in this historic session were, amongst others, Alvin Lee, Pete Frampton, Kenny Jones, B. J. Cole, Albert Lee, Delanney Bramlett, Klaus Voorman and Rory Gallagher. 'With Jerry Lee Lewis,' Rory said, 'everything is different. He sits down at the piano, and the tracks pour out.'

As one track followed another, the musicians started to mix and mingle. Rory teamed up with Kenny Jones, Albert Lee and Pete Frampton for 'Music to the Man', 'Jukebox', 'Johnny B. Goode' and 'Whole Lot of Shakin' Goin' On'. Throughout the session, Lewis looked for ideas for tracks. The old favourites were in the can, and he wanted something a little different. Someone suggested the Rolling Stones.

'Okay, which track?' Lewis asked.

The musicians proposed 'Satisfaction', to which Lewis demanded,

'Which one's that?'

He didn't know it. The others, flabbergasted, ended up laughing, whereas Lewis was furious. He sincerely thought they were teasing him. His anger grew when he found out that the song did actually exist. He made everyone leave the studio apart from Rory, whom he had read correctly. Rory wasn't one of the arrogant, conceited crowd you met in London. Alone with him, Lewis suggested that they work on the song together, and asked him to write out the words. On reading the lyrics and grasping their connotations, Lewis exclaimed, 'They got to Number One with that, and I got myself arrested for bullshit!' Calming down, he asked for an electric piano to be brought in, rehearsed the song, called back the musicians, and after a cursory once-over, they recorded. He hammered the keyboard with his feet and came up with a good cover, which was later to appear uncut on volume two. During the same recording session, Lewis attacked Kenny Jones from the Faces. As ever, Kenny was elegant, wearing a tartan jacket. Jerry considered him better dressed than himself, something he could not tolerate. Delanney Bramlett then suddenly arrived into the studio with a bottle of bourbon, which was actually forbidden. Lewis, however, hit the bottle, and once again, in a fit of moodiness, got angry with the musicians over something trifling, and made them all leave the studio. All except Rory. Making the most of the break, Donal came into the studio to modify something on Rory's amp.

Jerry, catching sight of him, asked him what he was doing there, to which Donal replied, 'I'm fixing Rory's amp.'

'Right, if you're with Rory, that's fine.'

Jerry sat down at the piano.

'It's a shame you're not doing any of your country tracks,' commented Donal.

Cut to the quick, Lewis aggressively replied, 'You're far too young to know anything about country music.'

'The first record I ever heard on the radio was Guy Mitchell's "Singing the Blues",' said Donal.

At that, Jerry started playing the first few notes of the song, and suddenly, perking up, he was back in a good mood. He decided to record the song, called the musicians back, and asked Donal to provide some backing vocals. A great respect had been established between Jerry and Rory by the end of that rather epic recording session. Some time afterwards, Rory was on tour in America. The group were to play at the Civic Hall in Santa Monica, and in the town, at the hotel,

*Rory, RTL recording studios, Paris*

huge posters of Rory had been stuck up, along with posters of Jerry Lee Lewis, who was playing his country repertoire at a small venue called the Roxy. Lewis invited Rory to his concert, sending complimentary tickets, and Rory, having the evening off, went along with Donal and Tom. On welcoming them, the club's manager, Mario, told them not to sit in the main theatre, as it would be packed, and moreover, with country fans, there was often a bit of trouble. He told them that he had a private box reserved for VIPs and that they were welcome to sit up there. Donal explained that Rory didn't really like sitting with the guests of honour, and would rather be with the rest of the audience. As they went to sit down, Mario added that he had some other guests coming later, and that they would love to meet Rory. 'OK, we'll see about that later,' Rory replied.

The show began. The first half was a country group – cousins of Lewis – and his son Lovely (who was later to die in a car crash). Lewis finally arrived on stage an hour late, and not, apparently, in top form. He sat down at the piano, fixed his mike and played his first few chords. As he was finishing his second song, his guests made their entrance, which did not go unremarked, for amongst them were John Lennon and Yoko Ono. Rumours had been escalating for several days that the Beatles were about to split up. Turning their eyes away from the stage, the entire audience shifted round to look at Lennon. Lewis started his third song, to complete indifference and in the general hubbub provoked by Lennon. Livid, Lewis changed the words of his song, throwing in some particularly vulgar lyrics, of which the least offensive were, 'Me, I'm far better than the Beatles'. Lennon leaned across the balcony towards the stage and shouted at Lewis, 'I don't like the Beatles either, that's why we've split!' But with the noise of the piano, although Lewis saw that Lennon was talking to him, he couldn't hear what he was saying. He thought that Lennon was returning his digs and insults, and his bad humour turned into anger. In his rage, he pushed the Steinway piano into the audience. A fight broke out in the ensuing chaos. There was complete panic. Rory, Donal and Tom were in the thick of it, and although Donal suggested that they go back to their hotel, Rory refused. 'All musicians have their bad days, when they feel tense and down, and Jerry Lee's feeling bad,' he said. 'It's when your friends feel bad that they need your support.'

Rory decided to go and find Lewis in his dressing-room. Tom borrowed Donal's backstage pass and accompanied him. Whereas Tom got lost in the wings, Rory managed to make his way, without any hassle, to Lewis's dressing-room, only to discover him sitting on a chair, his head between his legs and a glass of bourbon in his hand. Rory talked to him, managing to calm him down. 'You know,' he said, 'Lennon is a fan of you and your music. He didn't come here to insult you. When he talks about you, it's with respect.'

Listening to Rory, Jerry Lee was just starting to relax when the dressing-room door opened and Lennon made his entrance. His appearance stunned Lewis, and he thrust his hand into his bag, looking for something to throw at Lennon in an attempt to alleviate his anger. Rory leapt up and stood between them, grabbing Lewis' hand and reasoning with him while explaining the reasons for his anger to John. Just when things had calmed down and both men had accepted the misunderstanding, the door opened once again and Tom came in. His eyes moved from Rory to Jerry Lee Lewis to John Lennon. He gulped, took a piece of paper and a pencil from his pocket and landed in front of Lennon, saying, 'For me, you're the king of rock and roll. Would you give me your autograph?'

As Lewis rolled his eyes, Lennon took the paper and pencil and signed his name. Lewis was bright red, apoplectic with rage. Rory stood motionless. Tom, who hadn't a clue what had been going on, carefully put away the precious autograph. Lennon then asked to borrow Tom's pencil and paper, and moved towards the transfixed Lewis, knelt down on the floor in front of him and declared, 'You're the king of rock and roll. I've been waiting for this moment for twenty years. Would you give me your autograph?'

This Lewis did, more or less graciously, and as Lennon got up, the two men fell into each other's arms, hugging and congratulating each other. Rory breathed again. His role as mediator had prevented things deteriorating. Rory didn't enter any further into conversation with Lennon, not wanting to annoy Lewis, who was back in good humour once again. Thus, Lennon was the 'special guest' who had wanted to meet Rory. John and Rory didn't know each other very well. Lennon had been to two Taste concerts, at the Marquee, and had made eulogistic comments about Rory to *NME*. 'I've heard a group called Taste,' he'd said. 'Their guitarist is wicked!'

# LIVE IN FRANCE

The Belgians like their chips and beer – and their coffee. The Moka-bon Café is found on a little street in the centre of Ghent. Little old ladies with face powder, ravishing secretaries and spotty students were all to be found there, having a coffee while savouring a waffle topped with whipped cream. Ghent is a marvellous place, bourgeois, traditional and old-fashioned, harbouring at that time a dubious population of musicians, writers, painters, cartoonists and actors who frequented the bistros, sampled the bread and cheese and watched black-and-white films at the cinema. They added life and soul to the town.

Seated at a table in the Mokabon, Noeghan ordered another coffee and waited. He was there to see Roland, from the Blues Workshop. When the latter had called the previous evening to arrange a meeting place, he had not hidden his surprise.

'What?' he said. 'Do you know the Mokabon? How on earth are we going to recognise each other?'

'You don't know what I look like, but I know what you look like,' Noeghan reassured him.

Roland, of course, was late. The door opened and he came in, wearing a crushed-velvet jacket, light-coloured jeans and a floral shirt, a guitar in his hand and a travel bag on his shoulder. Noeghan got up and waved at him. They smiled at each other, shaking hands. An adventure had begun.

The first full national Rory Gallagher tour of France, in May 1974, was organised by Belgians. Ludo Debruyne, head of Lion Productions, and a partner of Ludo Marcello, suggested that Noeghan accompany the Rory Gallagher Band during their tour of France. Debruyne had asked him to cover Status Quo's French tour the month before. This time he asked Noeghan to take his car and pick up Roland, who would support Rory and his band. Noeghan accepted without hesitation. Amps and guitars – one electric, one acoustic – were piled

*Handwritten note with Rory's address, given to Jean-Noel Coghe*

up on the back seat of an old Citroen parked in the bright sunlight of Ghent's main square. Noeghan and Roland transferred them to the boot of the BMW. 'Someone will come and get the car,' said Roland, not worried about putting money in the meter.

They hit the road around lunchtime, driving to Metz, where they were to meet Rory for the first concert. Not long into the journey the two men clicked. Roland was anxious, despite the fact that he was a folk singer and had played with other folk singers, such as Tim Hardin and Martin Carthy, and even putting the musicians up in his home as they played throughout Belgium. He was impressed by Rory, and held his music in great esteem, but knew nothing about the man himself. Noeghan filled him in.

Late in the afternoon, they arrived at the novotel in Metz. Even before checking in, Noeghan decided to introduce Roland to Rory, who was resting in his room. Noeghan knocked on his door. Rory answered, welcomed them in. Noeghan introduced Roland as the support act. Rory bade him welcome, with his usual warmth and courtesy. One had to pass the test in order to be accepted. There was no pretence. After some talk about music and guitars, Rory suggested that they go down to the bar for a pint and a game of pool. The rest of the group – Gerry, Lou and Rod – came down to meet Roland, then headed back to their rooms until the concert. This tour, which began on 17 March 1974, was not supported by any radio station or magazine. The eight of them – the four group members, Donal, Ludo Marcello, Roland and Noeghan – travelled in two cars, a rented Mercedes and the BMW, with two trucks in front, one carrying roadies Tom and Steve, the other with Belgian lighting technicians. The first concert had been organised by Evapop at the Palais des Sports, with almost 1,500 spectators and two local support acts, Licorne and Nucleus. Roland was on after these bands, arriving alone on stage with an air of nonchalance, guitar slung over his shoulder. He plugged the jack into the amp as the audience asked themselves who he was. His fingers ran over the neck of his guitar from top to bottom. The sound fused, with echo. It was 'Galactic Glides', a track Roland had written years previously. The effect was hypnotic. The audience let themselves go, completely enthralled. Such a stylistic effect was to be found again later, with Roy Buchanan. Roland's acoustic guitar worked for rock, but more especially for blues and folk. His tracks followed each other back to back with rare mastery, and the audience were under his spell. In the corner of the auditorium, at the door leading to the dressing-rooms, stood an even more attentive group: Rory and his band. Rory stayed right to the last song, spellbound. When Roland left the stage, Rory made his way toward him, extending his hand in congratulations. This was sincerely meant, and was no empty gesture. Roland had passed the test, setting the seal on their friendship.

Roland, in turn, was fascinated as Rory climbed on stage for a set that lasted just under three hours and was packed with energy and emotion. Much later, the group found themselves in a restaurant, and were joined by their roadies and technicians in one big happy family.

To get to Lille from Metz for the next day's concert, they crossed Luxembourg and Belgium, to make the most of the motorways. The weather was good, and the cars travelled in convoy, not always respecting the speed limits. Rory accompanied Roland and Gerry in Noeghan's car. After crossing the French border at Wattrelos, Noeghan took them all to his usual haunt, Aux Amis, where an informal reception had been prepared for them. The place was full, and the young people welcomed Rory with warmth, everybody tasting the freely flowing local beers, Rodenbach and Gueuze, as Michel the waiter juggled glasses and bottles. Noeghan stopped again later on the way to Lille, at the offices of the local newspaper, the *Nord Éclair*, where he worked freelance. Another reception had been arranged, and in the entrance hall nearly a hundred fans awaited Rory's arrival. Rory was to remember these moments years later.

The concert, which took place at the Rotonde in Fâches Thumesnil, on the outskirts of Lille, had been organised by Albert Warin. It was also an enjoyable get-together, as many of Noeghan's friends came to what turned out to be a spectacular concert. One friend, despite having his foot in plaster, hammered the ground to the frantic rhythm of the music. On stage, the band were on fire, oozing flair and precision.

With Rory, everything came from inside. He had so much to express, and had the power to transmit these emotions to his musicians. As his accomplices, they reflected sensations that struck the audience like arrows in the heart, and they moved to Gallagher's rock, blues and acoustic tracks. He did sing, and his unmistakable voice was at one with his guitar. 'At the beginning, I stayed on stage for forty-five minutes. Now, I'll stay there for more that two and a half hours,' he commented.

It was an unforgettable moment of extreme emotion and unrelenting tension. When the other musicians left the stage and Rory picked up his acoustic guitar, the audience showed their joy. Rory was one of the few musicians who possessed the ability to break into the rhythm of a concert in such a way. When he got out his mandolin for 'Going to My Home Town', the crowd went mad once again. Sharing the same moment, the people clapped their hands and stamped their feet. For some of them, the Rory Gallagher Band was more rock and roll than Taste. 'Which isn't exactly true,' Rory said. 'We don't do any covers such as "Jailhouse Rock" or "Rock Around the Clock" on stage. The most important thing for us is to play Rory Gallagher music.'

This music was the child of rock and roll and black blues. But surely rock was also born from the folklore brought to the United States by Irish immigrants? And is the situation in Belfast not similar, to a certain extent, to that in Harlem? Segregation is not always a question of colour. Gallagher's music was a perfect reflection of everyday life: of anguish, and yet of hope.

When he left the stage, Rory would be exhausted. He would go back to his dressing-room, sit down in silence, sip a Coke and recuperate, stroking his guitar. He would say, 'We don't play like the rest of them, eh?'


## SWIMMING POOL


The next day, Sunday, was a day of rest. The French were going to the polls to vote for a new president of the Republic. Driving along the northern motorway, heading towards Paris, Noeghan explained to Rory, his passenger, that President Pompidou had died on 2 April, a day that had also marked the beginning of Status Quo's French tour. Because of the president's death, the tour was disastrous. Concerts had to be postponed or cancelled due to national days of mourning, which varied from town to town, depending on which day suited them best. After such a shock, the nation turned to introspection, and Status Quo attracted on average only four or five hundred people to their concerts. Rory appeared to be truly put out by Status Quo's bad luck; in fact, the two groups were represented by the same agency, Quarry Productions ('Quarry' for 'Quo' plus 'Rory'!)

They arrived in the early afternoon at their novotel in Survillers, about thirty kilometres outside Paris. The hotel was full of life. In France, not only do people vote on Sunday, they also celebrate First

Communions, with families getting together for the occasion. It was a hot day, and the children invaded the lawns, followed by adults in shirt-sleeves. A ball appeared and a kick-around began. One by one, the band members joined in, before all diving into the pool. Rory and Donal had a great time, fighting in the water like two kids, or two brothers.

In the bar that evening, between games of pool, Rory asked about French politics, the elections, and what was at stake in them. He brought up the situation in Ireland, which concerned him.

After dinner, they organised a party, stocking up on beer before the bar closed.

*Donal and Rory in the pool*
*(below) Rory relaxes playing pool*

Donal brought a radio cassette player down from his room, and Rory provided the music: the Dubliners, Planxty, the Chieftains – groups and musicians that he held in high esteem. They talked, drank and told stories, laughed, played pool and listened to Irish music. And, as in the Irish legend, they spent 'a third of the night recounting the heroic acts of the Fianna, a third of the night telling stories, and a third of the night resting'. Noeghan left them to it and headed back to his room. The next day he got up at about 7 am and bumped into Lou and Rod in the corridor. They were just going to bed.

Monday afternoon had been set aside for press conferences. Rory had played several times at the Olympia, to great public acclaim, but the French critics considered him to be lacking in charisma. Claude le Gac, Polydor's press agent, brought with him a handful of journalists – those who deigned to travel the thirty kilometres out of Paris.

By late afternoon, France had chosen a new president of the Republic. Giscard d'Estaing began his term of office as the Rory Gallagher group got moving. That evening Rory recorded a concert for the radio station RTL, in their cosy studio. About fifty people made up the audience, a lively public who appreciated Rory's dynamism. Whether in front of fifty or fifty thousand people, Rory always gave his all, and the concert was excellent, despite being interrupted by advertisements.

By 10 pm, it was in the can. Later, in a neighbouring restaurant, Rod told Noeghan about a Native Indian friend of his in America. He had been invited into their tribe along with his wife, and their marriage had been celebrated according to local custom, in a ceremony that lasted two weeks.

Lou Martin was delighted because the group were to visit Spain. To his own mind, he was of Spanish blood. He said Martin came from Martinez, and was very excited at the prospect of playing under Franco's nose. Rod claimed to be of Belgian descent. Ath is a Belgian town, from where one of his ancestors apparently set off to conquer Britain with William the Conqueror. After being knighted, he was subsequently called 'de Ath'.

The group headed back to their hotel at around two in the morning, getting a puncture at the toll-booth in Survillers. Early next

*Rory during a radio recording session for RTL*

morning, before leaving for Dijon, Noeghan got up to fix the car. He had his breakfast in the bar, served by a blonde waitress. She recommended a garage a few kilometres away, which was near her home. As she was at the end of her shift, she suggested that she go with Noeghan, and he could drop her off at her house. In the car, she told him that she had never heard of the Rory Gallagher Band. Suddenly, she decided to come with them, took three days off work, packed a bag and joined Noeghan.

'You'll never change,' Rory said to him, although he was quickly reassured. Corinne was not a groupie, and quickly not only became indispensable for her sense of organisation, but also became a friend. They hit the road again. Rory travelled with Noeghan up front, not talking for hours, staring ahead, lost in his thoughts. Together they drove hundreds, indeed thousands of miles like that, barely talking. Occasionally Rory would suggest they put on some music. He preferred Vince Taylor, whom Noeghan knew well, and he would ask questions about him. Noeghan also introduced him to the music of Maxime le Forestier. Rory listened attentively, appreciating his music and wanting to know more about him. He told him about the times Maxime would drive up to Lille in his old Renault 16 with dodgy headlights, Alain le Douarin in the front passenger seat, Patrice Caratini and his sidekick in the back seat.

Just outside Dijon, Noeghan left the motorway and made a detour via Beaune et Les Hospices. Rory and the others were delighted. 'It looks Flemish,' one of them said. In fact, Lille's Vieille Bourse, which dates from around 1600, inspired many other buildings of that period.

In Dijon, the novotel looked just like all the others. After they checked into their rooms, they usually played the game of working out what was different from the previous hotel: 'The toilet roll is on the left, yesterday it was on the right!'

Generally, as soon as they arrived in the hotel, Rory would close himself in his room, to read and rest; perhaps watch television, sometimes seeing one of the others. That trip, it was Noeghan who visited him. Before the tour, Noeghan had bought a second-

*Food on the motorway*

*Refreshment on the motorway*

hand Nagra tape recorder, which allowed him great freedom in recording. Rory had a good look at it, and then picked up his acoustic guitar, which was lying on his bed. Noeghan turned on the mike as Rory played a few chords. Afterwards, they went for dinner, in the hotel restaurant. Rory always had something to eat before each concert, at around 6 pm. Steak and chips, salad or sandwiches, depending on the mood, all washed down by a Coke, coffee or cup of tea. The others, musicians and roadies, would often join him before heading to the venue.

The Palais des Sports was a large venue, although it wasn't known for its great acoustics. At the end of the concert, dozens of young people waited to see Rory at his dressing-room door. As ever, he welcomed them warmly, listening to them, signing autographs and allowing them to take photographs. All went away delighted.

The next day they were to play in Lyon at the Palais d'Hiver. A cordon of police cars surrounded the venue, with helmeted officers on patrol. Rory was annoyed to see such a police presence, and regretted the fact that their deployment would probably only serve to further fuel any potential violence. About a thousand people came to see Rory that night, whereas only about a few came simply to cause trouble.

Events followed their usual course. The night was short, and the group hit the road early the next morning. As they left their novotel in Lyon, beside Satolas airport, the roadies had already left for Châtellerault. They had a long day ahead of them: eight hours in the car on A-roads. They crawled along the ring road in the sun, but managed to get through the Fourvière Tunnel without too much difficulty, and stopped for lunch in a truckers' café. It wasn't particularly pleasant, and the other diners stared at them strangely, with the kind of surprise that could easily have turned into aggression.

After the pre-concert sound check, Rory tirelessly tuned his guitars in his dressing-room, as he did every evening. He repeated this sacred ritual religiously. Seated in a chair, with his bag at his feet, he changed the strings and cleaned the necks. He carried out these

*Eating before moving to
the concert venue*

gestures conscientiously, almost as a sort of meditation, occasionally allowing himself a rest. He would joke with one of the others, have a bit of a laugh, open a can of Coca-Cola. Next, he would finalise things with Tom, and ask Donal a few questions. He would plug in his small amp and tune up with Gerry. Rod would already have his drumsticks in his hands, whereas Lou would still be holding his glass.

That evening, there were just 600 people in the audience. The local promoter explained that there were national examinations to be held the next day, but this didn't affect the quality of the music. Rory was on stage for almost three hours. When he left the stage, he would head back to his dressing-room and catch his breath, sitting down with a towel around his neck. He would stay like that for ages, silently unaware of the commotion around him, roadies coming and going, promoters chatting, the first curious onlookers arriving, guests picking at the cold buffet which was set out before each concert yet was rarely touched by Rory. Finally, he would get up and change his clothes, preferring to freshen up after the concert. Rory never changed his style to perform on stage. Waiting fans would then be welcomed into the dressing-rooms. Sometimes he would even pick up his guitar and play a little. This post-concert ritual could last for more than an hour, and therefore it was often difficult to find a restaurant that was still open. The kitchens would be closed; the chefs would have gone home, even when the promoter had booked ahead. The group had to be content with whatever they found, but Rory and the others did not make any particular demands. Rory was so amiable that even the grumpiest waiter would smile and do his utmost to ensure satisfaction.

*Novotel menu, signed by Rory, Gerry, Lou and Rod*

That night was short, with only two hours of sleep before leaving for Nantes. Arriving at the Parc des Expositions, they encountered a complication. The equipment was still in the trucks, and a sum of 80,000 French francs was being demanded – an unacceptable surcharge for the hire of the venue. Until they handed over the money, they would not be allowed to unload their vans. After a bitter exchange, they were finally granted a compromise: they were offered an alternative venue – a hall resembling an aircraft hangar – for a less outrageous fee. The public who were gathering outside the main hall accepted the change of venue without grumbling. Backstage, everyone was on top form, pitching in to help the roadies. The stage was set up without too much delay: the fatigue and difficulties had a motivating effect. In his dressing-room, Rory was doing an impressive imitation of Status Quo's guitarist,

Richard Parfitt, mimicking his onstage behaviour, his guitar at his side, copying Parfitt's poses and facial expressions as well. It was hilarious.

The last date of Rory's first French tour was a fantastic concert at the Alhambra in Bordeaux. Rory called Roland on stage for the third encore, the pair of them launching into a seemingly endless, delirious jamming session. This final jam between friends marked the end of the French leg of the tour, before they went on to Spain. The farewell dinner had a special feel to it. Everyone got together in a Spanish restaurant, probably for a bit of local colour in preparation for the days ahead. The end-of-tour atmosphere was relaxed, and Rory, laid-back and cheerful, was releasing all his tension. He chatted and laughed, ate and drank.

The stories poured out, and they partied, as the in-house guitarist serenaded them. They invited him to join them, and raised a toast, while Rory picked up the guitar and started to play. It was already

*Bordeaux May 1974. End of the French tour, Rory in fine form during the post-concert dinner*

95

late by the time they went to a nightclub in the town. Lou Martin was in a surprising state. Perfectly upright, he was holding his glass firmly in his hand. It was never the same glass, as he alternated beer and spirits. Suddenly, he called Noeghan, handed him his glass and collapsed, only to pick himself up again with dignity and take his glass back. 'Thanks Noeghan,' he muttered, before knocking his drink back.

When they left the nightclub it was already morning. On arriving back at the hotel, Rory, Gerry, Roland, Lou, Donal and Rod headed towards the bar and asked the breakfast staff for beer, before starting a game of pool.

Rory invited Roland and Noeghan to follow them to San Sebastian for the first concert of the Spanish tour. Roland, with a heavy heart, had to turn down Rory's offer. He couldn't go with them, as he didn't have his passport with him. He stayed in the hotel, awaiting Noeghan's return.

Rory travelled with Noeghan, eyes fixed on the road, listening to music. The customs officer at the border was fastidious. Long hair always seemed to attract mistrust, despite – of perhaps because of – the fact that Rory's posters covered walls fifty kilometres away from San Sebastian.

Rory's arrival was a major event. It was the first time the town had received such an important artist. Spain had opened up to rock groups the previous year, but only the cities were affected. At the hotel, a palace overlooking the bay, about twenty radio and news-

*San Sebastian. Poster on walls, announcing Rory's concert*

*Gerry, Rod, Rory and Lou on stage in San Sebastian*

paper journalists were pacing up and down, waiting for Rory. He had barely arrived before he was confronted with a barrage of questions in an unexpected press conference. The organisation of the gig was flawless. Miles away from France, there were two thousand people in the huge hall where the concert was to be held. Two thousand people determined to break free and have a wild time. The police cars patrolling the streets, the armed soldiers ready to intervene, were forgotten. The concert was incredible, with a perfect rapport between Rory and the public.

Once again, the night was long – or rather, short. Early in the morning, Noeghan asked for his bill at reception, only to discover that Rory had beaten him to it and paid for him as his guest. When he went into the dining-room for breakfast, another surprise was waiting for him: Rod and Lou, their eyes heavy with sleep but with smiles on their faces, asked him to come and join them at their table. They had wanted to get up and have breakfast with him. A few hours later, they flew to Madrid and Noeghan drove to Bordeaux, where Roland was waiting for him at the novotel. They headed for Lille, then Belgium. The kilometres flew by: they had covered thousands of kilometres over the last ten days. In Tourcoing, at 2 am, a kilometre away from the Belgian border, a drunken driver ignored the right of way, and drove into them.

*San Sebastian bay; from left to right: Rod de Ath, Rory, Gerry McAvoy, Lou Martin*

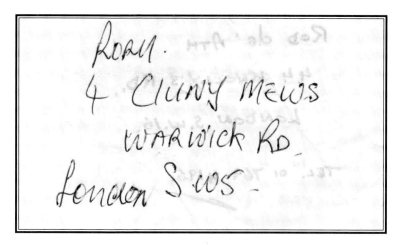

*New address handwritten by Rory for Jean-Noël Coghe*

# IRISH TOUR

Rory made his way along the quayside. A small fishing boat, followed by a horde of screaming seagulls, was coming back into the port, its motor spluttering and giving off a strong smell of diesel. With his denim jacket over his shoulders, Rory walked purposefully towards the lit-up shopfronts. He stopped, raised his head and read the sign: 'Michael Crowley'. Pushing open the door, he stepped into the shop, where guitars of all shapes and sizes were laid out everywhere. Michael Crowley stepped forward, his hand outstretched and a smile on his face. Tony Palmer, on camera, sought to capture every detail as he followed Rory, filming his rediscovery of Cork in a walk through the city. The children in the street had asked for his autograph and had followed him into the shop, where, since his departure, a plaque had been put up saying that Rory Gallagher had spotted his Stratocaster there.

Rory, Rod, Lou and Gerry toured Ireland in December 1973 and January 1974, a tour which became the subject of a film, initially conceived as a television documentary. This visit to Ireland coincided with a double live album, simply entitled *Irish Tour*, which came out in mid-1974. The French tour took place between the band's visit to Ireland and the release of the album.

'Ladies and gentlemen ... Rory Gallag-her!' He burst out on stage in his denim jacket, checked shirt, belted jeans and trainers. The audience were screaming as the raw, bright light swept the

*Rory on stage*

stage. Lou sat down at his electric piano, while Rod, a little tense, adjusted his cymbals. Gerry had assumed a fighting stance, one foot forward, ready to face the onslaught. Rory, his guitar slung over his shoulder, headed straight to the front of the stage, grabbing the jack that the ever-faithful Tom had been holding. Rory turned around to look at Gerry and plugged the jack into the amp. It crackled as he hit his first few chords, and with a quick 'Yeah', followed by a 'C'mon', he started to play, dazzling, indeed drowning, the audience with a shower of scintillating sounds. The public were transfixed. With a hint of a smile on his inscrutable face, tight-jawed and leaning forward, he would suddenly leap towards the mike, throwing his head back, holding his guitar like a machine-gun firing out violent, piercing notes in bursts. He would look towards Gerry, whose eyes never left him, anticipating his next move. The tempo would change, and Rod, concentrated and conscientious, would hold it all together. Lou, as if sitting on hot coals, would jiggle and gesticulate, shaking the long black hair which masked his face, striking chords and notes which enveloped and complemented the insane sounds coming from Rory's guitar. Rory criss-crossed the stage, his face dripping with the beads of sweat that gathered on his forehead and ran down his cheeks, mixing with his tears, falling on his guitar. When he flung his head back, the drops of perspiration would fly from left to right, his guitar shining, caught in the spotlights, polished with drops of silver that then fell to the stage. He would move as if in a dance, avoiding some invisible object, spinning round towards his musicians, spurring them into action with just a look.

They kept their eyes on him, ready to follow his next improvisation as he lifted his guitar high like a trophy, his sword of light. Such complicity, such telepathy: Gerry knew exactly what Rory was going to do before he did it, but Rory also knew when Gerry was going to play. No signals, no signs. Gerry explains why they were so close: he was originally a solo guitar player, and in fact, his fingers were too short to play bass as it should be played. He played it as one would a guitar. Rory, however, enjoyed playing bass. They understood each other's instruments, and so they understood each other. They were in each other's minds, each other's souls. Such alchemy was magic, a fusion of two master musicians. As 'Cradle Rock' came to an end, with resounding applause and screams, Rory presented his line-up to the public: 'On bass guitar, Mr Gerry McAvoy ...' and so on. He then laid down his guitar, took off his jacket, armed himself once again with the guitar and announced the next song, 'I Wonder Who', by Muddy Waters. After a moving version of 'Tattoo'd Lady', the crowd picked up the chorus, counting from 91 to 100, with him, then without him, in 'Too Much Alcohol'. On acoustic guitar, he paid homage to Tony Joe White by playing 'As the Crow Flies'. 'A Million Miles Away' showed the sensibility and controlled tone of Rory's playing, and he demonstrated his impressive dexterity in 'Walk on Hot Coals'. Rory's slide guitar in 'Who's that Coming' electrified the audience. 'Back on My Stompin' Ground' (the tour ended in Rory's home town of Cork) and 'Maritime' (the club, of which Van Morrison was one of the founders, was a base for Rory while he was living in Belfast) are the two bonus tracks on the album. *Irish Tour* captured all the fire and emotion that Rory gave out on stage.

Some of the tracks were recorded by Ronnie Lane's mobile recording studio (which only turned up for the last concert at Cork's City Hall, due to the intensity of the Troubles in the north at the time) and Donal's mixing desk. Two tracks from a jamming session, recorded during studio work, complete the album. The documentary produced by Tony Palmer was distributed throughout the world. A video and DVD of the film has been produced, with the sound remastered.

*Rory on stage*
*Liège 1976*

# THE STONES

Night was falling in Zaventem, Brussels. The taxi parked in front of the departure hall of the airport. Four guys emerged from the car, bags in their hands. One of them had a Nagra recorder on his shoulder. The one holding the tickets urged them to hurry up as they made their way to the check-in desk. Dirk de Vries, press agent with WEA Belgium, had invited three journalists to accompany him to Stuttgart, where they would spend a few hours in the company of the Rolling Stones, as well as attending one of their concerts and a reception. The Stones were on a European tour, with several concerts planned in Belgium and one set aside especially for the French. They had been banned from France. One of the airport employees watched their progress, his arms folded. Dirk handed him their tickets. The man stared at him, imperturbable, and smiled. 'Strike,' he said. Three days later, the same group found themselves in front of the same desk, this time headed for Copenhagen. The Stones weren't in concert but were holding a party in one of the hottest clubs in the Danish capital, with tight security, guests frisked at the door, a free bar and a racy live act. The journalists, queuing to get in, were each clutching a red, white and blue penis made of wool: their entrance ticket.

Previously, journalists had been allowed to meet the Stones one at a time. Mick Jagger, sitting down at a table, answered Noeghan Jelcoe's questions in perfect French. Keith Richards, watching logs burn in a massive fireplace, with Bill Wyman and Billy Preston at his side, was happy to be interviewed. Charlie Watts made some jokes, while Mick Taylor, Brian Jones' successor, sat on his own in a corner, unsmiling. He looked rather preoccupied and gloomy. He left the band at the end of that tour, forcing them to look for a replacement.

Rory was in Cork, spending time there resting after his last tour before going to Japan, Australia and New Zealand. One day he received a telephone call from the Netherlands. It was the Rolling Stones calling him from Rotterdam, asking him to join them in a studio session, where they were recording the album *Black and Blue*.

'I said OK,' explained Rory. 'But once I got there, there were some technical problems with the studio. I was supposed to be there for a week, but with the delay, I only had two or three days. I absolutely had to get back to London for the Japanese tour. In the end, I played with them for two nights, and we had a great time. In fact, it was

GREETINGS FROM JAPAN,
WE HAVE JUST COMPLETED
A VERY SUCCESSFUL TOUR
HERE. NEXT WE GO
TO AUSTRALIA FOR
TWO WEEKS. HOPE TO
SEE YOU SOON. BEST
WISHES  Rory + Donal.

MR. J.N. COGHE
D/7 PRESIDENCE DES JARDINS
20 RUE DE MENIN
7700 - MOUSCRON
BELGIUM.

*Postcard sent from Japan by Donal to Jean-Noël Coghe*

more like a jamming session – we didn't do anything precise, like "Here's this song". And I really liked Keith Richards as a guitarist.' The track Rory played on was called 'Miss You'.

He refused to sell his soul for a commercially acceptable career. He didn't want to replace Eric Clapton in Cream (Taste and Clapton had the same agency, and had toured together) and he did not intend to become the fifth member of the Rolling Stones. The Stone musician he appreciated most was Brian Jones, and Jones' death bothered him. Rory was in his own way the epitome of a rolling stone. He began his second tour of Japan, a country he thought was fantastic for musicians.

'They like and appreciate all sorts of music,' he said. The tour went on to Australia, and to New Zealand, where he played for the first time.

## BASTILLE

In the midst of all this, Rory came to France during a European tour. When in Europe, he would always take Roland with him as the support act. They played in Holland and in Germany together, where Rory was a permanent guest of the Rockpalast, and he played there seven times – something of a record! They also travelled together to the United Kingdom, Ireland and Switzerland, for the Montreux Festival, where again Rory was regularly invited, and had been asked to play with Albert King. Rory also took part in the recording of the track 'As the Years Go Passing By', where he plays the first solo, which figures on Albert King's 1977 Montreux *Live* album.

The concert in Paris took place in the old Bastille railway station, which had become a temple of music. The organiser was a new member of the clan, Pascal Bernardin (whose father founded the Crazy Horse night club in Paris), head of his own production company, and a faithful friend to the group. He was later to co-ordinate all of Rory's French tours. At that time, Rory had a contract with Polydor. His albums were selling well, and those in charge of the French company did their utmost for Rory. It had even been announced that the director himself was to come to the concert. On stage that afternoon, Rory was busy doing soundchecks. During the rehearsal, Noeghan suddenly came up with an idea. Rory was a fan of Maxime Le Forestier, who lived only about 400 metres from where they were, on the Boulevard Henri IV. Noeghan had been to Maxime's house on a number of occasions, where of course they had talked about Rory. The opportunity was too good to be missed. Noeghan went up to Catherine, took her by the hand and whispered, 'Come with me, I'm going to fetch Le Forestier.'

Catherine followed him, and in a few minutes they were in the courtyard of the building in which Maxime had an apartment on the ground floor. Luckily, he was at home, with a number of friends. Noeghan told him about his idea, which Maxime was to accept without hesitation. Dropping everything, he decided to join the party. Together, they made their way to the Bastille, arriving at exactly the same time as the director of Polydor, Monsieur Kerner, who couldn't believe his eyes! Maxime was also signed to Polydor, and sold a lot of records. Polydor's boss couldn't get over it,

'Maxime, is that really you?' he asked, knowing that Le Forestier was not exactly known for his appreciation of rock music. It was inexplicable; the marketing people certainly hadn't planned it. Maxime, not at all taken aback, told him that he was there to see a friend, as he lived nearby. In fact, he had never met Rory, who was already in his dressing-room, and welcomed Maxime with pleasure. After Roland's performance, Maxime took his place in the concert hall, where he sat down on the floor in front of the stage. He stoically witnessed two and a half hours of rock and blues, and couldn't but marvel at the ease, dexterity and finesse with which Rory played his acoustic set. At the end of the concert, Maxime saluted Rory and discreetly made his way out. It is well known that the friends of our friends are indeed also our friends.

That evening had a party feel to it. All the musicians, technicians and roadies ate together at a restaurant near Les Halles, Au Pied du Cochon, at what was only the beginning of their night out. Pascal Bernardin then took the whole group to the Crazy Horse, owned by his father, where they were expected, as guests of honour. The girls were not shocked by the unadulterated enthusiasm they provoked: they must have been warned! At least it was a change from lecherous businessmen taking out their clients, or their mistresses, for a few cheap thrills.

## HÉLIN

He had repeated his story a hundred times: how he, a dedicated fan of Taste, had walked forty kilometres to Dourges to see them in concert at the beginning of their musical career. One day Noeghan promised him that he would take him to see Rory the next time he was playing in the north of France. A few months later, the opportunity presented itself. Staying for three days in Belgium, Rory was to play at Les Halles in Courtrai. By an incredible stroke of luck, that very evening, twenty kilometres away, Maxime Le Forestier was playing at the Colisée in Roubaix. Noeghan made his plans, organising a group dinner at the end of both concerts, which Rory and Maxime both accepted. Everything was running smoothly, and Noeghan invited Marc Hélin and a few other friends. For the entire week preceding D-day, Hélin was in a state. For a man who was very fond of a drink, he swore that on the day of the concert he would not touch a drop. 'I want to make a good impression on Rory,' he said.

On the day itself, Noeghan met up with Le Forestier in Roubaix. Coming out of the Grand Hotel, they bumped into Hélin on his way out of the office. Hélin, with a tired step and his head in the clouds, didn't even see them as he made his way towards them, a towel under his arm. Noeghan called out to him, and he stopped in surprise. Suddenly, coming back down to earth, he caught sight of Noeghan, and the hairy and bearded person at his side. Overcome with emotion, he pointed his finger at Le Forestier and spluttered, 'Lou Martin'. He was in such a state of excitement that he was confusing Le Forestier with Lou, Rory's hairy, bearded keyboard player.

Maxime was rather surprised and taken aback, until Noeghan explained the situation, scowling at Hélin. Maxime smiled at the mix-up, while Hélin sheepishly muttered a few incomprehensible phrases and went on his way, saying he would see them later. That evening, Hélin turned up exactly on time. He hadn't a beer all day, and didn't want anything to drink, categorically refusing when he was offered a pint. On their way to the concert, he once again repeated his story of his long walk to Dourges.

On arriving in Courtrai, Hélin was given a backstage pass, the magical ticket that would allow him access to the dressing-room where Rory was tuning his guitars. Rory welcomed Hélin with his usual courtesy. Hélin, with tears in his eyes, and mumbling excitedly, shook Rory's hand, attempting to explain, in faltering English, his memories of Dourges. Rory smiled as Hélin fished from his pocket some old, yellowing photographs, cut from a magazine, which Gallagher had autographed.

'Do you remember?' he kept on saying. It was all a very long time ago for Rory, but he didn't disappoint his visitor by contradicting him. Pointing out the array of food and drink that had been laid out, Rory offered him a beer, but was turned down. Hélin, with a sparkle in his eye, kept his promise, although he was longing to accept. He also bumped into Rod, Gerry and Lou, who greeted him warmly. He was in seventh heaven.

The house lights dimmed as the stage lit up, with Hélin seated in the front row for what turned out to be a fantastic concert. It was almost midnight by the time Rory and the others left by a side door of the huge complex where the venue was situated. Alongside the building was a small lake, which, due to wintry weather, had almost frozen over. Everyone was walking quickly to get to the warmth of the cars, with Hélin in tow. Walking along the water's edge, Hélin, not looking where he was going, turned to Noeghan and said, 'You see, I didn't draw attention to myself, I didn't act like an idiot!' only to fall promptly into the lake!

Everybody, including Rory, Donal and the band, was alarmed, and rushed to help him. With water up to his waist, soaked to the skin and with dripping hair, Hélin gathered himself together and declared, as if nothing had happened, 'Well, the water's cold!' at which

*Backstage: Roland, Rory, Gerry, Lou*        *Rod, Gerry, Lou*

everyone burst out laughing. They pulled him out of the water, and Rory opened his bag, handed him a towel, a dry pair of jeans and a jumper, and told him to dry himself off and get changed, but Hélin refused to take them. He couldn't possibly have worn Rory's clothes; he had too much admiration for the man. So he climbed into the car, wet and shivering, as if it were nothing at all. Noeghan drove off, followed by the band's car, arriving twenty minutes later at the restaurant, where Maxime and the musicians were waiting for them. Hélin, dripping wet, was a roaring success. Maxime and Rory were sitting opposite each other at the table, exchanging impressions of their respective performances and talking about music and guitars. Hélin, still soaking, sat down beside Noeghan and a mutual friend. When asked for his order by the waiter, he said, 'I'll have what he's having', pointing to the person seated next to him, without paying attention to what he had actually chosen. As the waiter served them their meals, however, he burst out laughing, saying, 'But I don't like pasta!'

In the small hours of the morning, the two groups went their separate ways. Maxime was going to Paris, while Rory headed back to his hotel in Courtrai.

Noeghan dropped Hélin back home, still wet. The next day, on discovering what had happened, his mother interrogated him about the state of his clothes, but she remained sceptical, refusing to believe him when he swore that he had had nothing, absolutely nothing, to drink. That episode remained etched in Rory's mind, and twenty years later, during his last meeting with Noeghan, he brought it up with a smile on his lips.

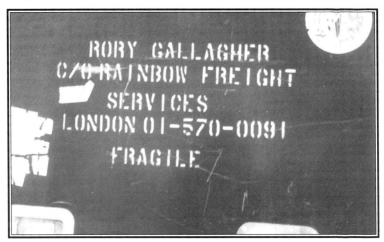

*One of the cases containing Rory's equipment*

# AGAINST THE GRAIN

Rory left Polydor and signed with Chrysalis. The music scene was changing, but Rory remained loyal to blues, rock and country. His album *Against the Grain*, which came out in 1975, did indeed go against the commercial grain, which only served to make it an even better album. Rory was on top form, and Lou, Gerry and Rod knew the ropes. Together they created a group in its prime. The album, which was recorded in London's Wessex Studios, opens with the impressive guitar and piano interface of 'Let Me In', followed by the jazzy 'Cross Me Off Your List', which reveals just how at ease Rory was in this genre. The melodious 'Ain't too Good' is next, before the powerful 'Souped-up Ford', with electric keyboard and piano. Rory often played this track in concert, its high-speed slide guitar inspired by his travels in a Ford Executive V6, which Muddy Waters had taken a shine to during his visit to Britain in 1973 for the recording of *London Sessions*. 'Bought and Sold' showed how Rory still hurt after Taste's break-up, a theme he comes back to in 'At the Bottom'. 'I Take What I Want' is a cover of the classic 1960s Sam and Dave track. Bo Carter, a member of the Mississippi Sheiks, one of Rory's favourite bands, wrote 'All Around the Man'. It features a splendid Lou Martin keyboard solo, with a thrusting beat and bottleneck guitar closely matched by the vocals. In 'Lost at Sea', Rory explores the theme of solitude. 'On the Western Plain' was written by Leadbelly, and was one of Rory's classic acoustic country tracks, played on his Martin D35 on stages across the world. 'Cluney Blues', a lively instrumental, and 'My Baby, Sure', a rockabilly track in the Carl Perkins guitar style, feature as bonus tracks on the album.

# UNPLUGGED

The aeroplane from London arrived as scheduled at the airport in Ostend, where, on the ground, there was a busy atmosphere. A special bus was waiting at the end of the runway for those on the private charter flight. Their passage through customs was aided by the presence of several officials, all rushing to lend a hand to the procession of passengers: Maggie Bell, Leo Sayer, Queen and other big names from the world of British show business, who were all very much in vogue – and were arriving in Belgium on a scorching hot day in July. Escorted by the faithful Tom and flanked by two acoustic guitars, Rory was also part of the group. Like the rest of his travelling companions, he had been invited by the Belgian National Television Company to their Lions d'Or ceremony, which celebrated the careers of musical artists. The viewers of BRT had voted Rory 'Musician of the Year'. The programme was to be filmed in public on the Belgium coast, at the height of the holiday season, with the participation of many carefree holidaymakers. Suntanned girls jiggling in suggestive bikinis hunted for autographs as the hectic television technicians installed the set. Although the programme wasn't being filmed live, everybody was on edge. Noeghan, watching the preparations and listening to the rehearsals, was also nervous. Tom asked him what time the next day's filming was to start. 'Early afternoon,' replied Noeghan, not terribly at ease in his new role as television producer for the French channel FR3.

Maurice Delbez was definitely not a programme director like any other. As a filmmaker, he was the author of several entertaining, unpretentious films, which were rather commercial and were described by well-informed critics as 'flops'. These films included *À Pied, à Cheval et en Voiture* (On Foot, On Horseback and By Car), with Darry Cowl. Delbez was promoted and moved to Lille to work in television and radio production. Lille's FR3 station was by no means regional, although it was considered as such by Parisians. In fact, it had great potential, for the four million inhabitants of the Nord Pas de Calais region included the youngest population in France. What's more, the signal didn't stop at the border, for beyond that imaginary line lay a population that shared the same roots, the same ancestors, despite the language barrier that existed between the French-speaking Walloons and the Dutch-speaking Flemish. Thanks to cable television, which had been available in Belgium since the 1960s, the station's signal covered all of Belgium. Delbez, working with Noeghan at FR3, accepted the latter's proposal to broadcast a programme about Rory Gallagher. Noeghan, who knew about BRT's filming, suggested that they make a twenty-six-minute documentary that was dedicated solely to Rory and would interpret his acoustic repertoire. It would have been impossible to film the entire band, due to budgetary limitations, so Noeghan would concentrate solely on the artist himself. The project was accepted, the date was fixed, the studios were booked and the crew was mobilised.

It was break-time in Ostend. All the artists were to eat together on a terrace built especially for them on the seafront. BRT did things in style. Noeghan was sharing a table with Rory. The table next to them was occupied by Queen. Brian May was a friend of Rory's, and had already met Noeghan. He was surprised to learn that Rory was not to travel back to London with them. Rory told him that he was going to Lille for another television broadcast. Noeghan told him it was a regional production, to be broadcast later in twenty-one other regions. Brian May told Noeghan that Queen were interested, and would like to do the programme, only to be informed by Noeghan that the budget for it was non-existent. A performance would usually have cost 5,000 French francs. 'No problem,' replied Brian, as if at an auction, giving his telephone number to Noeghan, who scribbled it onto a bit of paper. Even at that price, however, FR3 refused to film Queen! As for Delbez, after the Rory Gallagher programme he was given his marching orders. So much for public service.

Once the filming was over, Rory, Tom and Noeghan drove to a Holiday Inn hotel in the town of Lille, where they spent a calm evening before heading straight to bed. Roland and Catherine met up with Noeghan the next day, just before lunchtime. They all went to pick up Rory and Tom, and made their way to the Lambersart recording studios. A number of technicians' vans were out ready for filming, and heavy cameras were sitting here and there in the yard.

The director was Jean de Nesle. His wife, Yvonne Sassinot de Nesle, was a well-known costume designer for period dramas. They lived in a farm in French-speaking Flanders, where no doubt to this day you could find the very same Rory Gallagher records that Noeghan bought and lent them during the run-up to the programme. De Nesle was a jazz specialist and blues lover. He even brought along his vintage American-style car for some of the shots, in one of which Rory is seated on its bonnet, his Dobro in his hand. The takes were filmed in the studio under normal recording conditions, before the

*Rory during the filming of FR3's 'unplugged' session, Lambersart studio*

technicians would intervene, with a multitude of different shots of Rory. A few days previously, after a suggestion from Noeghan, they had filmed some footage in the run-down streets of the old town, Vieux Lille. Since then, this area has been rebuilt, and the population, mainly poor and marginalised groups who had been paying a modicum of rent, was chased out. The restoration pushed up rents tenfold. It turned out to be quite profitable, the feather in Lille's cap. Lille's sister towns, Ghent, Courtrai and Bruges, had never required such renovation, however, for they had always been kept in good condition. The idea was that Rory would be shown the footage, which he obviously had not yet seen, and he would then improvise on guitar and harmonica. The final shot would be of a cat staring into the camera. The street on which they were filming was Rue des Vieux Murs (The Street of Old Walls). Rory liked the project, and Catherine, in her role of one-time photographer, took as many photographs as she could. In very different surroundings, in a different situation, Rory demonstrated his mastery on acoustic guitar, slide and Dobro.

The technicians, who were usually fairly blasé, were overcome by Rory's talent, kindness and courtesy. Recording started, one shot after another, without any hitches. Sometimes parts were done twice, or Rory was interrupted and asked to redo his intro, usually due to a recorder that didn't quite switch on in time. Rory, smiling, would stop and wait until the problem was corrected and the loudspeaker told him recording was about to begin again. A beep would sound and the red light would come on as the first chords were struck and Rory's voice rang out. It was a wrap.

At the end of session, at about 5.30 pm, one of the administration staff turned up. He asked Rory to sign a form, and in return gave him a cheque for 5,800 French francs – the fee for his participation – drawn from a French bank. However, it was Friday night, all the banks were closed, and at that time, exchanging money was not an easy process. It took six months before Rory managed to get the money from the cheque.

Not long after Rory's death, Noeghan became concerned about the fate of the film. In fact, it had been destroyed in the flood that soaked all the tapes stored in the cellar at the Lambersart Studios. Miraculously, a copy had been made by their commercial department, checked in and registered at the archives of the National Audiovisual Institute in Lille, and forgotten about. Once Noeghan proved he had been the producer, the Institute gave him a copy of the film.

*(Top) contract drawn up by FR3 for Rory's TV recording session, July 1975, a programme produced by Jean-Noël Coghe*

London contact:
Carole Brown
484 King's Road
Chelsea
London, S.W.10.
telephone (01) 352 0082

28th January, 1976.

Mr. Jean Noel Coche
D7 Residence des Jardins 20,
Rue de Menin,
7700 Mouscron
Belgium.

Dear Mr. Coche,

We would be most grateful if you would confirm with your bank the arrangements made for the transference of funds to London bankers reference Rory Gallagher, as David Oddie's office are still not in receipt of the payment.

Please do not hesitate to let us know if you have any problems.

Yours sincerely,

Carole Brown.

*(Bottom): letter from Rory's management to Jean-Noël Coghe, worrying about not having received payment (January 1976)*

Once the filming had ended, Noeghan organised a dinner party in his flat. His wife, Martine, was on holidays in the south of France with their godson Michael, and so he had to requisition a few friends to help him prepare the meal. Régis loved Ireland and had been there several times. His partner, Dany, was originally from the Beaujolais region of France. Noeghan had recently accompanied them on a visit there, and left over from the expedition were roughly a dozen bottles of Fleurie wine, a few of which were decorating the table. The atmosphere was relaxed and friendly. Roland and Catherine felt right at home, as Tom and Régis chatted about Ireland, Noeghan and Dany worked in the kitchen, and Rory spotted an Elvis Presley LP, a twelve-inch from RCA that included the songs 'That's All Right Mama', 'Blue Moon of Kentucky' and 'Moving On'. And so the dinner began, with Presley in the background. Elvis was one of Rory's favourite musicians. Rory, although he had the soul of a bluesman, had the heart of a rocker. He had much admiration for the King, his character and personality, and his sense of professionalism. Two lithographs of Elvis hung on the walls of his apartment. Into the frame of one of them he had slipped a concert ticket dated 1976. The lithographs were two beautiful works of art by David Oxtoby, and represented Presley at two stages of his life. (Ironically, David Oxtoby had started a portrait of Rory when he was still with Taste, but never finished it!)

There were certain similarities between Rory and Presley. Their temperaments led them to close themselves off from the world and lose themselves in their music, outside of which they felt completely lost. The drugs prescribed to them by their doctors led both of them to their nemesis. As Rory held the Presley album in his hand, how was he to know that his music would figure alongside the King's, on an

*Lithograph of Elvis Presley (with concert ticket) hung on Rory's wall*

*Rory borrows the jacket of an admirer and poses, hair swept back, as the perfect rocker*

*Promotional CD from BMG/RCA bringing together Elvis Presley and Rory Gallagher tracks*

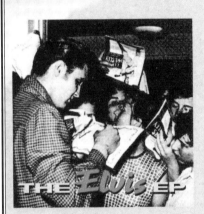

Elvis "Artist Of The Century" has become the most successful campaign ever on Elvis' back catalogue. One of the highlights of the promotion was the August release of four outstanding Elvis mid price collections: Ballads, Country, Movies & Rockin'. A track from each of these exceptional albums is available on "The Elvis EP".

The promotion of the lavishly re-packaged classic albums of Rory Gallagher continues. To date we have released ten of his classic albums at mid price plus the highly successful "Etched In Blue" sampler on Camden.

August saw our first full price Rory album "BBC Sessions", four tracks of which feature on "The Rory Gallagher EP".

Sales across the catalogue released to date are now in excess of 400,000 units.

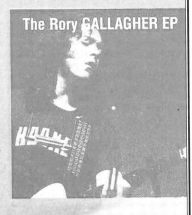

album uniting their music. He even had the look: once, coming out of a concert in Belgium, a friend handed him a 1950s-style jacket. Rory tried it on, combed his hair back, smoothed down his sideburns and changes his look. His expression changes; he stretches out a finger and strikes the pose. A pose which all adolescents, all rock fans, have attempted, standing in front of the mirror in their parents' bedroom. A rock attitude.

The bottles came out one after another, and the Fleurie was fresh, fruity and lively. Buddy Holly followed Presley. Noeghan told the story of the time when they were offered the opportunity to write to American pen pals. He accepted, and soon received a long letter, with photograph, from a young, very WASP-like person in Arkansas. Noeghan wrote straight back and asked him to send him a Buddy Holly record which he couldn't find in France, and their correspondence stopped right there! Rory, amused, looked at the album cover of *Reminiscing*. He had painted a copy of the face when he was twelve.

# GHENT FESTIVAL

Around 11 pm, the empty bottles started to pile up, and as they opened the last one Roland suggested that they go to the party in Ghent. In the middle of July, Ghent was the epicentre of an extraordinarily lively festival. Thousands of people invaded the streets, bistros and an immense podium, on which was erected an effigy of the late-nineteenth-century Flemish poet and left-wing sympathiser Karel Wari. In his time, the people of Ghent spoke French, and Flemish was reserved for the workers and peasants, the proletariat. One hundred years later, the population was having a great time, and Karel, with a happy face, watched proudly over the rejoicing crowd, who lifted their heads to him. Alcohol was flowing freely; although its sale was actually illegal, bottles were hidden under counters and whiskey was served in port glasses, just like in the time of the Prohibition. During the day, the streets were packed with kids drawing on the pavements, decorating the roads, and cars were banned. In Ghent, Roland was well-known, and recognised. As he walked around the streets, taxi drivers, bus drivers and tram drivers alike all sounded their horns to greet him.

They arrived in the middle of the packed crowd gathered in front of the stage, where a group was playing, Roland and Rory both shook

*Rory, Ghent Festival, 1975*

*Ghent Festival, 1975, Roland and Rory*

118

hands with people around them. Whispers became rumours, circulating through the crowd from row to row, reaching the people on the square, under the trees, on the terraces of the cafés, becoming louder and more insistent: 'Rory Gallagher and Roland are here'. People turned towards them, patting them amicably on the back, and little by little, the crowd opened up and the two men were carried off, swept by the tide of people, to the foot of the stage. Cries were heard: 'On stage, Rory!' Everyone was urging them, and they could not resist. They climbed the steps onto the stage as the other group stopped playing, the musicians greeting Rory and Roland as the crowd called out for them. Guitars changed hands, and Roland's musicians, who had been separated from them in the audience, joined them. Tom checked the amp Rory's guitar was plugged into, and the music rang out beautifully under a starry sky, accompanied by the ovations of thousands of people, singing, dancing and clapping their hands to the pulsating rhythm of the group. It all lasted a very long time – indeed too long for our friend Tom. Like the rest of them, he had enjoyed quite a bit of Beaujolais, which, along with the fatigue of the last few days, got the better of him. He fell asleep on stage, on top of the plug-box! He was so ashamed that he still laughs about it today when people remind him of it; a moment etched in the heart and memory of all those present that evening, the jamming session at the Ghent festival.

The party ended as the sun came up. At around 6 am, Noeghan drove Rory and Tom back to their hotel in Marcq, only to waken them again at 11 am to drive them to the airport at Zaventem. Their flight was at 1 pm, and they set off on time. They had only been driving along the motorway for a few minutes when Rory, who had been sitting in silence in the front seat, suddenly turned to Noeghan and said, 'I'm sorry, but I'm not feeling good.' The car pulled over onto the hard shoulder, Rory got out, was sick, and climbed back in the car again, his face white. Thirty kilometres down the road, Rory, getting paler and paler, said, 'Noeghan, we've got to stop.' This happened three or four times. On reaching Zaventem, they saw a plane taking off: the plane bound for London. They had missed it. Tom went to change their tickets, and booked seats on the next flight. As they had plenty of time, they went to the restaurant for a bite to eat, and to settle Rory's stomach! They set the guitars down on the floor. Amongst the stickers on one of the cases was 'ZZ Top'. Noeghan had heard some of their music, and loved it: it was very rock-and-blues. ZZ Top were hardly ever played on the radio.

'La Grange,' said Rory. 'They're Texans. I've toured with them, and they're great.' Not long afterwards, during a television broadcast with Slade, Noeghan asked Decca's press agent, about these Texans. 'Oh yes, ZZ Top.' He went to his car, opened the boot, and handed Noeghan a LP. 'Here, this was sent to me from the States, but I'm not sure whether we'll bring it out in Europe or not.'

Noeghan took the LP, with its red-and-black cover. It was *Fandango*, ZZ Top's third album. Two weeks later, Noeghan bought their first two albums, in Dallas, Texas.

## LONNIE DONEGAN

The van drew up in front of the building. The driver got out, opened up the back door of the truck, lifted out some drum cases and rang the doorbell of Donal's London office. Rod's drum kit was to undergo a few changes before an important concert. On 23 December 1975, Rory was playing the last date of his British tour at the Royal Albert Hall, with Roland as his support act. As Donal talked to the technician, he realised that he knew Donegan. In fact, it was Lonnie Donegan's old drummer. Lonnie Donegan, their childhood and teenage hero, without whom they wouldn't be who they were that day! Apparently, Lonnie had already left the music world some time before that, and had been keeping himself to himself. His former drummer, who had remained in contact with him, told Donal that Donegan was presently in London. Things then happened very quickly. Donal decided to invite Lonnie Donegan to Rory's concert, which would be a huge surprise for him. Without telling Rory, Donal contacted Lonnie, who accepted his invitation. That evening, Lonnie turned up at the concert, in black tie. This was a perfectly normal choice of outfit for the Royal Albert Hall, one of the most chic and prestigious venues in London, usually the home of opera and ballet. Upon seeing the public crowding in the doors, in their jeans and jackets, Lonnie Donegan was astonished. He wasn't familiar with the world of rock and roll, and felt nervous about entering it. Donal, who intercepted him immediately, reassured him. He suggested that Lonnie should go on stage and introduce Rory, who was completely unaware of the Christmas present that his brother was organising for him. Lonnie tentatively agreed, but solely on the condition that beforehand, Donal would introduce him to the public.

On leaving his dressing-room to go on stage, Rory guessed that something was up. He distinctly heard Donal introduce Lonnie Donegan, to the wild applause of the audience. Rory then stopped dead, on hearing Lonnie Donegan's voice over the loudspeakers, saying his name, Rory's name! He made his way to the stage, to the crowd, completely bowled over. Lonnie Donegan, his hero, the man who had inspired in him the love of and passion for music, was there in front of him, standing beside Gerry, Lou and Rod, looking towards the wings beckoning him, Rory, the pupil, to come to the master, his mentor. In shock and moved to tears, Rory ran on stage and joined him, to the cheers of the public.

*Rory, before a concert*

After such a moment of intense emotion, Lonnie Donegan took his place in the audience, beside the representatives of Rory's record company. On leaving the concert, Rory discussed with the head of Chrysalis the possibility of releasing one of Lonnie Donegan's albums, which would help revive his career, and Rory was keen to produce such an album. What a happy honour for Rory, and indeed, some time afterwards, Lonnie Donegan did sign a recording contract with Chrysalis, although it was Adam Faith who actually produced the album, in 1978. Ringo Starr, Elton John, Ron Wood, Brian May, Zoot Money, Leo Sayer, Nicky Hopkins, Mick Ralphs, Jim Keltner, Klaus Voorman, Rory himself, and many others took part in the recording session. He played guitar on three of the ten tracks on the album: 'Lost John', 'Drop Down Mama' and Lonnie's classic 'Rock Island Line'. Rory took great pleasure in playing with Lonnie, but was disappointed not to have helped in producing the album, as had been originally intended. It was a disappointment he would never forget, for he would have loved to be totally involved in the recording. Donal later pursued Rory's idea, releasing a Lonnie Donegan CD on the CAPO label. *Muleskinner's Blues* brought together Van Morrison, Albert Lee, who had participated in the 1978 session, and Chris Barber, with whom Rory had recorded and in whose famous Chris Barber Band Lonnie Donegan had played in 1949. Buddy Holly's drummer, Jerry Allison, was also there, along with Gary Brooker and Jacqui McShee. Although nobody drew attention to the fact, Rory was spiritually in the studio too.

*Rory and Donal, 'it's time'*

*Gerry and Rory tuning their guitars*

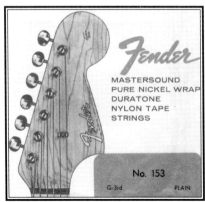

*Type of Fender string used by Rory*

*The two guitars used by Rory, the Telecaster on the left, Stratocaster on the right*

# CALLING CARD

The album title *Calling Card* was also the title of a track that demonstrated the cohesion and complicity that held the group together, all with steady rhythm and continuous piano–guitar dialogue. *Calling Card* is a flirtation with jazz, a genre in which Rory excelled. The album was recorded in Musicland, Munich, in 1976. After so many tours in Germany, Rory ended up recording there. He felt much happier in Germany than in London. Deep Purple's bass player, Roger Glover, produced the album with Rory. The two groups had regularly played together in America, and the two musicians shared a closed friendship. This influence can be heard in 'Moonchild', a classic track with biting guitar. 'Do You Read Me' is the opening number, with a powerful, upbeat tempo. 'Country Miles' is an intense piece of slide guitar, while 'I'll Admit You're Gone' is a finely chiselled acoustic track. 'Secret Agent' is much meatier: a lover of B-movies swears that his companion, his accomplice, is a secret agent. All hell breaks loose to outbursts of guitar and drums. Rory, a great fan of John Le Carré, carries it off with style. Look out for the harmonica. 'Jacknife Beat' and 'Edged in Blue' are slightly unusual and very gentle. 'Barley and Grape Rag', on Dobro, with harmonica, a heavy bass, and brushes, is a recreation of country blues. This album is a true gem. The remastered CD has two bonus tracks: 'Rue the Day' and 'Public Enemy' (B-girl version).

# DYLAN

In 1977, after *Calling Card*, Rory became the first artist to make a televised performance for Rockpalast, via Eurovision, which was broadcast to 100 million viewers, excluding France. That year, he started his tenth tour of the United States. At the end of the tour, he was to play at the Shrine Auditorium in Los Angeles, which, as Donal had been warned, had a rather bad reputation for regular thefts of instruments, particularly from the dressing-rooms, and guitars had been stolen on more than one occasion. As a precaution, Donal placed two security men at the dressing-room door, under strict instructions to let nobody in. There was a huge crowd for the last concert, in the auditorium and in the wings. All the managers from Chrysalis had made the journey to come to the party that the company had organised in Rory's honour. Rory had accepted, stipulating that Donal supervise.

When Rory left the stage, he was completely worn out. He was resting in his dressing-room as one of the two backstage bouncers came to find Donal, to tell him that there was a guy insisting that he had to see Rory. Rory, who did not particularly want to leave the room, asked Donal to go and see him. Donal did so, and told him how tired Rory was, but that if he were to wait half an hour, he could go in and see him. He explained that Rory liked chatting to the people who came to meet him after a concert but that this was a bad time. The man said that he understood but that he would have really enjoyed talking to him about acoustic guitar, and his style, but that it was OK. He turned to go when suddenly something clicked in Donal's mind. Right from the start of the conversation, Donal had been saying to himself, 'I know this person' – but lots of people at the time had a Bob Dylan look about them, a bit like Ian Hunter from Mott the Hoople. As he looked more carefully at the man walking away from him, Donal wasn't sure. As the man went downstairs, Donal saw his profile. He had a moment of realisation. The vision he had in front of his eyes superimposed itself on a vision of an album cover with Dylan's profile. It was the same profile. The evidence was right in front of him: not just a sneaking suspicion, but Dylan himself walking away! Donal swore to himself as he realised just what he had done. He dashed down the stairs and caught Dylan, saying, 'I have to shake your hand, and I'm not letting you go!'

Donal didn't know what to do. He didn't want to appear hypocritical to Dylan, who hated that. He didn't want to say, 'Forget everything I've told you.' So instead, grabbing the other man's hand, he led him upstairs and opened the dressing-room door. 'Guess who wants to see you?' he asked Rory, guiding Dylan into the room. Rory was flabbergasted. Donal, not very proud of his blunder, left them alone. A little shaken, he joined Tom downstairs, and discovered the awaiting mass of journalists who had been following Dylan. This was his first public appearance since his motorbike accident. Meanwhile, up in the dressing-room, Rory and Dylan, later joined by Donal, talked about country blues and Blind Boy Fuller. Suddenly, someone came in. It was Terry Ellis, the boss of Chrysalis. He approached Dylan, who looked him up and down and said to Donal: 'How come he can walk straight in, and I couldn't?'

Donal, ill at ease, searched for an excuse. 'He's been waiting for a while, and he's the head of the record company,' Donal said.

Dylan's harsh attitude towards the visitor astonished him. He found an explanation for it some years later, however, while watching a film (*Don't Look Back*) about Dylan's visit to Britain. Dylan was debating philosophy with some students in a university. They held a very different position to his, didn't share the same opinions and disagreed with him. One of the students, more vehement that the others, continually contradicted him. Donal discovered that the student was none other than the future head of Chrysalis. After all those years, Dylan had recognised him immediately, and did not hide his aggression, implying that he had not forgotten the debate.

Rory and Dylan had no more contact for a while. Rory went to one of Dylan's concerts in London but didn't manage to get past the bouncers. They wouldn't allow him up to the dressing-room! In 1991, Donal received a phone call from Dwarf Music, Dylan's publishers. They asked him for the album *Live in Europe*, with the track 'I Could've Had Religion', a favourite song of Dylan's, and one which he was considering recording for his acoustic album. Over in the United States, Rory's record company had apparently informed them that they didn't have the album. Donal sent him the CD of *Live in Europe* and included Rory's most recent album, *Fresh Evidence*. Not long afterwards, Dylan sent the brothers a fax to thank them, and to tell them that he thought *Fresh Evidence* was great. He told them he was sending over a copy of his last album, *The Bootleg Box*. Rory dreamt of working with Dylan. As at that time, Rory Gallagher and Bob Dylan shared a similar style, on stage and in recordings. *Fresh Evidence* strengthened this link. The opportunity to perform together presented itself in 1994 when Claude Nobbs, the organiser of the Montreux Festival, called Rory.

Claude Nobbs suggested that Rory play on the same evening as Dylan. In fact, Dylan was to play at 7.30 pm; he hadn't wanted to go on after Rory. When Dylan came off stage, between the two sets, he sent his head of security to Rory's dressing-room to tell him that Bob said 'hello', but as he didn't want any hassle from security, he was sending a messenger to warn them of his visit. Donal was stunned: nearly twenty years on, and he hadn't forgotten! The truth was that Dylan was hiding behind the door: he burst into the room, very amused at his little joke. Donal offered to leave, as a way of excusing himself for his previous behaviour, but Bob insisted that he stay. They talked about everything – except music. Rory knew the names of all Dylan's children, and asked him how his family was doing. Donal asked him about the track 'I Could've Had Religion', which he had sent him. Dylan explained that he had recorded an acoustic album and had considered 'I Could've Had Religion', but that on later reflection, he realised that the song, performed repeatedly by Rory, had become Rory's song. His desire was to record traditional blues, but that track was authentic Gallagher. The song previously had only two verses; now there are four or five. He would have loved to include it in the album, but he would have felt that he was stealing something from Rory. To this, Rory immediately replied that he did not care in the least, that, on the contrary, he would have been flattered and would have regarded it as a seal of approval. They arranged to meet in New York, and to record the song together. This was in June 1994, a year before Rory's death. The planned meeting never took place.

After he was admitted to hospital, in the early months of 1995, Rory, to avoid falling into a depression because of post-surgical shock, was in intensive care and visitors were not allowed. However, the doctors agreed to let him see people who could perhaps provoke, by their presence, a positive reaction in him. On leaving the hospital, Donal came across a poster advertising Bob Dylan in concert, for one evening only, in a venue near the hospital. Donal tried to contact him, but with no success. On the day of the concert, Donal couldn't leave Rory's bedside to go to the venue. All his efforts to telephone him were in vain. Four days later, however, he received a telegram, addressed to Rory. It said quite simply, 'God bless you, get well soon, keep on playing' and was signed 'Bob Dylan'. Rory was delighted to receive it, for nobody knew that he was in hospital, nor did anyone know that he had an operation as he had not wanted people to know. He kept that telegram on his bedside table, where it stayed, right to the end.

In August 1995, after Rory's death, Dylan came back to play at the Phoenix festival. Donal thanked him for his telegram, which had moved Rory so profoundly. He offered to give him one of Rory's guitars, but Dylan felt he couldn't accept it. Donal explained that he didn't want it to end up hanging on the wall of some trendy joint and that Rory's guitars should remain in the hands of the musicians he loved, where they could be played. Donal then decided that he would offer Dylan one of Rory's guitars, at a concert Dylan was to play in Cork in 1997. By a twist of fate, Dylan had a heart attack that very day, and the concert was cancelled. One of Donal's greatest desires would be for Dylan to record 'I Could've Had Religion' on his brother's guitar.

# BIG BILL

In the summer of 1977 Rory went back to Ghent, where he played at the city's festival – officially, this time – with the rest of his group Thousands of people gathered in front of the stage to celebrate his presence, for he was practically an honorary citizen. Also, because everyone was expecting it, and everyone was hoping that it would happen, it did. Rory invited Roland on stage to play with him. Roland's arrival culminated in a massive jamming session on stage, where a rather plump, bearded and bushy-haired gentleman also joined them. He pulled out his harmonica and joined in. Big Bill, originally from Louvain, and a friend of Roland's, was quite an exceptional character. He had worked with Roland on occasion, and indeed Roland once joined Big Bill's band for a series of concerts, as he also did later with Va Ya Candidos, and another friend Arno, a member of Charles and the Lulus. The Roland–Big Bill line-up was so mind-blowing, so rock-and-roll, that Rory was completely seduced by them and demanded that they provide support for his upcoming Belgian tour.

Big Bill was someone out of the ordinary, larger than life. His real name was Armand Krakkebass. The day after the festival, after all the partying, he had an important gala. When his musicians came

*(L to r) Lou Martin, Roland, Rory and Gerry surrounding Big Bill, Ghent, 1976*

127

to pick him up, he was fast asleep and didn't quite seem to follow what was going on. He climbed on stage like a zombie, played for the duration of the concert, then promptly fell asleep again once it was over. On waking up the next day, he had forgotten everything. The only thing he could remember was that he was supposed to have given a concert the day before. Panicked and full of remorse, he called in each of the musicians to apologise for his absence! What's more, at the end of each concert, he would usually play the very first song of the evening as an encore. That evening, slightly tipsy, he came on and played the first song, thanked the audience and left the stage. He thought they were already at the encore!

As unpredictable as ever, he managed to cause a scene at Rory's concert in Louvain. Not realising the gravity of his actions, Roland gave Big Bill the keys to the locked dressing-rooms while Rory was on stage. Bill picked up his things, conscientiously locked the door, climbed into his car and drove off. No keys, no dressing-rooms! They finally managed to track him down in his favourite drinking den at the other end of town.

*Rory on stage, Arena Hall, Deurne, 1977*

# THE SAN FRANCISCO SESSIONS

After a long tour of Japan, Australia and the States, Rory and his musicians had a two-month stopover for a studio recording in San Francisco. Rory wasn't on top form, Gerry recollected. He was exhausted and hassled. The atmosphere on tour had changed. Gerry and Rory would share one dressing-room; Rod and Lou would share a different one. There was no real divide; this was just the result of the growing pressures on, and events happening around, the group itself. Rory, against his will, had been depicted as a rock star, and he was extremely popular in Britain, across Europe and in America: this popularity threatened to monopolise his existence. Rory the individualist, the solitary soul, was caught up in a whirlwind of fame. He couldn't go out for dinner, go to the pub or go out for a walk without being recognised. Always affable and polite, he was nonetheless embarrassed by the situation. Deep down there was a secret nostalgia for the band's first tours of the United States. Gerry reminisces about how, in 1971, the three group members and Donal would traipse across the United States in a station wagon, more often than not setting up their own equipment. Together, the four mates shared a very strong bond. Dissatisfied with the production and the recording, Rory took the decision to abandon the untitled album. He was alone in San Francisco. Gerry had gone back to Ireland to celebrate his birthday with his family. Rory was left with his demons. Worse, he

*Rory on stage*
*Liège 1976*

129

got his thumb shut in a taxi door, which prevented him from playing for a number of weeks. It was a difficult period.

## RUPTURE

The tape was running, and the loudspeakers blared out the tracks that were to be part of Rory's latest album. But in the San Francisco studio, Rory looked a little vague. He didn't like it, and declared that the quality wasn't good enough. He cancelled the session and came back to Europe, listening to the tracks that he hadn't liked. The group, as it had been evolving over the past five years, had reached the end of its natural life. You could almost feel the fatigue in the band. Lou and Rory had been together for a long time, and Rory was beginning to feel rather weighed down by his keyboardist's style. The structure of the album was very orchestrated, which made Rory feel trapped. He wanted to rediscover a sort of musical freedom, where he could explore the potential of other possibilities. But he was stuck, for he wanted a three-piece. It was nothing personal: Lou and Rod were his friends, and would remain so, but Rory always liked to try something new, and to play with different musicians. That was deeply ingrained in his character: as soon as he had mastered something, in his eyes it became less than perfect, and he questioned everything, in order to go even further. Always dissatisfied, constantly searching for the impossible, these characteristics were anchored in his soul. Lou and Rod understood, and drew back, playing together for a while, and sometimes accompanying others, such as Chuck Berry.

## SAINT-MARTEN

The River Lys flowed by peacefully, with lazy barges and tall trees. The village of Saint-Marten-Laten was hidden there, in the middle of the countryside and the stillness. A few kilometres from Ghent, it had always been a favourite haunt of artists. Flemish painters and writers went there for inspiration and retreat. The village became famous because, despite the fancy villas that had been built, the original little brick houses remained, preserving the authenticity of the village and its people.

Roland and Catherine lived in this village. A garden filled with flowers and herbs surrounded their home, which was built in the traditional Flemish style. The home was often filled with the couple's friends.

For many months Rory, and often Donal, lived there, welcomed by the couple. Rory had an upstairs bedroom and would spend hours in their living-room, rooting through the thousands of records – country, blues, rock and jazz – which Roland had collected. At the bottom of the garden, they had built a well-equipped recording studio. Rory would shut himself in there and work in solitude. He probably reworked the tracks they had worked on in San Francisco. He lived at the locals' pace of life, Roland and Catherine's friends became his friends, and together they frequented the cafés, restaurants and cinemas of Ghent – places where his music was played. Always closed off from the world, rather secretive and very discreet, Rory rarely came out of himself. This didn't prevent him from having a good time, or letting his hair down. Once Roland was searching the record shops for any albums of Gene Vincent that he didn't have. Rory managed to gather them all up without him realising, and offered the collection to him on his birthday. Noeghan would visit the brothers regularly. One day he drove Rory to Ghent, to get strings for his guitar. In the music shop, Rory talked to the owner about instruments, and tried a couple of guitars. Like an attentive pupil, he also listened, and was always open to learning something new.

They went to Brussels later that day, to attend an Eric Clapton concert at the National Forest. They arrived in time for the soundcheck, after which Rory made his way backstage to meet Ian Stuart, the sixth member of the Rolling Stones. Ronnie Lane was also there, playing with his band Slim Chance. Rory had recorded his album

*Catherine and Roland's house where Rory and Donal lived for a few months during their stay in Belgium*

*(Top left) Rory and Roland, rue de Gand; (top right) Roland and Rory, Music Shop in Ghent; (right) Rory tries out his guitar; (below) Rory in Jean-Noël Coghe's car … thousands of kilometres!*

*Rory and Jean-Noël Coghe with the car after a show, Brussels 1973*

*Irish Tour* with Ronnie's mobile studio. A few months earlier, Ronnie had left the Faces, snipping in the bud Steve Marriott's project to re-form the Small Faces, the band of their youth. Noeghan had toured with the Small Faces in 1966, when they were just eighteen years old. Ten years later, Stevie had told Noeghan about his project when he was still with Humble Pie. Kenny Jones and Ian McLagan, both members of the Faces, confirmed the plan. But Ronnie explained why he had refused: because you can never relive the past. The Small Faces reformed without him, and Ronnie went on to record with Eric Clapton and Pete Townsend, working on albums packed with emotion, before forming Slim Chance. Few of these details were ever known. Not long afterwards, Ronnie was struck down by illness: the multiple sclerosis that confined him to a wheelchair and was ultimately fatal.

Bill Wyman, Charlie Watts and Chris Rea came together to form Willie and the Poor Boys, working with Kenny Jones and Jimmy Page. They recorded an album and donated the proceeds to a multiple sclerosis charity in memory of Ronnie.

That evening, anonymous in the auditorium, Rory stayed to see Ronnie Lane's Slim Chance and Eric Clapton, as just another concert-goer.

## PHOTO FINISH

Back in the UK, Rory and Gerry auditioned drummers in a studio audition. London was brimming over with them, but Rory had little success. They were children of the disco age, couldn't hold a rhythm, didn't feel the blues and didn't understand rhythm and blues. Their engineer at Air Studios, Colin Farley (a drummer himself), suggested that they try a musician he knew, Ted McKenna, ex-drummer with the Alex Harvey Band. Ted was a perfect match; indeed, he hit the spot! The trio bonded quickly and left for Germany's Dieter Dierks Studio. Rory didn't want to record in London: the city oppressed him. So they fled, and settled thirteen kilometres from Cologne in a little town called Stumel, which had one hotel and two bars. There was a good-natured atmosphere about the place, which Rory loved and in which he felt perfectly at ease. He relished the fact that he could walk from the hotel to the studio rather than drive. It was a twenty-four-track studio. Rory had brought his own engineer over with him: Alan O'Duffy had also worked on the Rolling Stones' *Let it Bleed* and Paul McCartney's *Venus and Mars*.

The album was to be called *Photo Finish*, as a reminder of its last-minute arrival at the record company, and was completed in three weeks. Rory, having rejected 80 per cent of the album in San Francisco, had written new material, such as 'Shin Kicker'. According to Donal, 'Shadow Play' is a track which sheds light on Rory's double life, on- and off-stage: 'a little bit of Jekyll, a little Mr Hyde'. 'Cloak and Dagger' is like the B-movies Rory loved, with superb harmonica thrown in. 'The Last of the Independents', another cinema track, was written just after Rory read an article about the film *Charley Varrick*. Rory, in the world of music, was himself the last of the independents of his generation. 'Overnight Bag' is an acoustic piece, describing the loneliness of life on the road. 'Brute Force and Ignorance' is the story of a three-piece band. 'Mississippi Sheiks' was dedicated to the Southern blues musicians of the 1920s and 1930s; 'Fuel to the Fire' was another blues ballad. 'Cruise On Out' was penned with Elvis Presley in mind, with 'rockabilly' drums, punching bass and a guitar sound straight from Sun Records, all reworked after the San Francisco session. Neither 'Early Warning' nor 'Jukebox Annie', with Dobro slide and harmonica, was on the vinyl album.

Rory had wanted to remix the album before releasing it on the CD format. He never did. Instead, Donal contacted Colin Farley, the original engineer, who took on the remixing project, with the help of Tony Arnold. After *Photo Finish*, the trio hit the road almost immediately, on a world tour that was to begin in Europe. France and Belgium were among the first ports of call. Noeghan and Roland hooked up with them in Le Mans, where they met Ted McKenna for the first time. Nothing had changed in the Gallagher show: after lengthy and careful preparation, there was still the inspiring three-hour concert, an avid and curious crowd who would come to the dressing-room – and a hunt for a restaurant that was still open at that time of night.

## ON THE AIR

The telegram arrived just in time. That evening would be something, for on 10 October 1978, Rory's French tour brought him to Lille. He was to play at the Palais des Sports in a concert organised by Albert Warin. For the event, Noeghan was granted authorisation, all the way from national headquarters, to dedicate four hours of airtime on radio FR3 to the gig. Although it was a regional station, it reached right across to Brussels and down to the north of Paris. It had never been done before. They weren't just recording the concert, but transmitting it live, with all the hiccups, difficulties and risks involved. It required organising technicians, setting up heavy equipment, finding a budget and, vitally, obtaining permission from the most important person: the artist himself. The telegram was the confirmation. Rory was allowing them to record and transmit the concert. Otherwise, the programme could not have gone ahead, as they wouldn't have been allocated the money to make it. At that time, rock music was very much looked down on. But the battle was being fought and won, especially when rock musicians themselves took part in the combat. Rory was not the only one to allow his music to be broadcast; other musicians had also accepted, including Peter Hamill and Van Der Graaf Generator, Doctors of Madness, Ange and Magma, Kraftwerk, Maxime Le Forestier, Renaud and Veronique Sanson.

Noeghan brought out his heavy artillery. He was expecting the bigwigs from Phonogram in Paris, who distributed Rory's records throughout France, and felt that they, in the provinces, could make a better job of recording the concert than Paris would have done. Before the concert started, around 9 pm, an hour-long programme was dedicated to Rory's career. Noeghan had settled into the dressing-room next to Rory's, who hadn't arrived yet. It had been transformed into a studio, with cables criss-crossing the floor, microphones on the table, a bustling assistant and a technician waving madly to indicate that they were on air. For practical reasons, the signature tune and the records were being played from the control room, where another broadcaster and a team of technicians were ready. Good timing was all they needed. The other guests were huddled around the mike as Rory arrived. He said a few words before retiring to his dressing-room, as the pace quickened.

Backstage, things were hectic. Tom was everywhere at once. Gerry and Ted were looking on with amusement as Rory tried on a baseball cap. A technician adjusted the equipment that was pressing into Rory's back, and gave him a mike, which would allow him to move around freely. Gerry and Ted were waiting at the foot of the staircase that led onstage. Tom was setting out the guitars, switching on the amps and going through his last-minute checklist. At the mixing desk, Rory's technicians were ready. They were directly connected to the airwaves. The sound-checks they had carried out that afternoon were more than satisfactory. The radio technicians were in communication with the control room, where a final record was being played as they waited for the concert to begin. Smiling and relaxed, in his denim jacket and with his Stratocaster in his hands, Rory joined Gerry and Ted. He signalled to Noeghan, who joined them, and together they strode onto the stage. Noeghan took the microphone, for the listeners at home to experience what the audience could see, and later to cover over the radio silence between songs. Rory moved forward, to the screams and cries of the spectators. He plugged in his Stratocaster, with the throbbing bass and thumping percussion in the background, and music invaded the airways.

It was more than two hours before Rory left the stage, exhausted, his face dripping with sweat, his shirt soaked. He shared a few words with Noeghan before going back to the dressing-room, followed by the equally exhausted Gerry and Ted. In the darkness of the concert hall, 4,000 spectators were waving the flames of their cigarette lighters and calling Rory's name. The ever-vigilant Tom assessed the situation and reported back to Rory, who reappeared seconds later, to the screams of the audience. The band started their encores. It was midnight: the concert was not over yet, but the radio programme was. The event, in its incredible depth and emotion, was of an exceptional quality.

*Concert in Lille, 10 October 1978. From left to right: Gerry McAvoy (bass), Ted McKenna (drums), Rory (front stage)*

# GRUAGAGH

The Rory Gallagher Band later played at the Olympia in Paris, accompanied by Brian Auger Trinity, and it was a sell-out. The concert started normally enough, but after the first few numbers Gerry's bass amp cut out and he was left pretending to play, as if nothing was wrong. Rory, picking up on the problem immediately, started to play more and more intensely to compensate for the lack of bass. No one in the audience was any the wiser.

Another time on tour in Ireland, Rory and his musicians turned up in Galway for one of several sell-out concerts, only to discover that the local promoter had got his dates mixed up, and instead of

*Rory at the Olympia*

137

there being thousands of people in a packed venue, there were only thirty-odd. Unmoved, Rory played a show anyway, as he'd always done, whether for an audience of one or for a thousand and one, and returned to play the next night to a full house.

The Belgian National Television studios were rather dull, with their artificial lights and oppressive atmosphere, nonchalant technicians sitting on the feet of their heavy cameras, munching sandwiches or drinking beer during the long waits between takes. The production assistant was taking notes in a corner, while the presenter laughed heartily at some joke. The musicians came in and were studied from afar by the staff. The cameras were put in place, under the director's orders. Guitars were plugged in. The musicians, motionless, waited patiently for the signal. A few orders were shouted out, a bell sounded, the red light flashed, and the music burst into life, hitting the shell-shocked technicians.

'It was as if we had just come out of a grey fog, only to be dazzled by thousands of lights,' said Erik the photographer. They were transported, blown away, as a warm feeling came over them. Then, suddenly, it stopped, before they even realised what had happened. They looked at each other in astonishment. The lights went out and the grey fog returned – along with the mediocrity. Rory came and Rory went. A little bit of his magic stayed behind, however, in their hearts.

Although every time Rory came into the studio with new material, the new songs were always complete, Gerry had never seen him take notes of any kind. The inspiration for his work often came from adventures and anecdotes from their time on the road, more often than not during their numerous American tours. 'Daughter of the Everglades', which recounted their time in Miami, Florida, was a classic example of this. Rory liked to plunge deep into the heart of the American byroads, seeking out surprising little clubs where he could jam with local musicians, soaking up the authentic climate and atmosphere. Gerry remembered one particular incident when they were touring close to New Orleans, deep in voodoo country, and Rory dragged them into the bayou, armed with his guitar. During the jam session that inevitably followed, Gerry recalls a riff that Rory came out with that particularly impressed him. It was five seconds of pure genius and emotion that Rory was unable to repeat a few minutes later at the instigation of Gerry. The moment of instinctive, automatic improvisation was gone and could not be recaptured. This was often the case with Rory, be it on stage, in rehearsal or in the studio:

he would let fly with passages of such intense beauty that it was impossible to reconstitute them on command. There was no mystery; it was quite simply magic!

Roy Rodgers has said the same thing about the blues guitarist John Lee Hooker. Rodgers, a producer, who himself was a blues musician, explains: 'He would just come into the studio, sit down with his guitar, and suddenly start coming out with some amazing stuff. The recording equipment would not yet be on, and none of it would be on tape, lost forever to posterity.' Rodgers would be mortified, but Hooker, unmoved, would already have passed on to something new. Roland, who was born in the town of Boom, had met the creator of 'Boom Boom', at home, in San Francisco, and during the ensuing conversation, he freely admitted that he held Rory in very high esteem.

Gerry considers Rory to have been one of the three best white blues guitarists of all time, along with Eric Clapton and Jeff Beck. All three men were, undoubtedly, outstanding technicians, the difference was, in Gerry's opinion, that Rory not only played the blues but lived, breathed and personified the blues: they were his life.

To love the music as he did, Rory naturally had a passionate relationship with the guitars he played, and he built up an impressive collection of over 150 of them – including famous makes such as National, Fender, Gretch and Burns, to name but a few – during the course of his life. As Gerry once said, however, 'Whatever the colour, make or age of a guitar, in Rory's hands it would automatically become an exceptional instrument. Rory could do what he wanted and produce his own, unique sound from any guitar.' Leaning lovingly over the instrument, his long hair would fall free over his shoulders, encircling his doll-like face, a smile playing across his lips.

## TOP PRIORITY

Be warned, this is an explosive album! It is Rory at his best. The aggressive guitar-playing on 'Follow Me' sets the pace. 'Philby' is based on Englishman Kim Philby, who spied for the Soviet Union. Between that man's life and his own, Rory draws several parallels of living on the edge, always ready to take to the road at a moment's notice, to run, making no ties or romantic attachments. The track features Rory on an electric sitar that he hired from Pete Townsend. 'Wayward Child' and 'At the Depot' are rock numbers, as is 'Bad

Penny', which is coloured by the spirit of the south. 'Just Hit Town' is another semi-autobiographical song, documenting through rapid, powerful and insidious guitar riffs Rory's continual flight from one country to another, never deviating from his inevitable destiny. 'Off the Handle' is a fierce blues track, as are 'Keychain' and 'There's No Escaping from the Blues in Your Soul'. 'Public Enemy' is a tribute to the B-movie detective heroes of Rory's youth. Included on the CD version are two supplementary tracks recorded in the Dierks Studios in Cologne. 'Hell Cat' is a blues–rock number, and 'The Watcher' is a track that features heavily the bass guitar and drums, giving it an unusual sound quality that Donal refers to as 'surf rock'. At the time when the album was being recorded, Rory's reputation in the United States was firmly established and his record company was generous with its promises. The title of the album, *Top Priority*, is a sly, humorous reminder to them of this fact. Rory's humour could be as fierce as his guitar-playing.

## PRIVATE LIFE

The ideas behind the Kim Philby story preoccupied Rory. He spent his life on the road, working towards his chosen aim, never creating ties nor having a place to call home. He lived out of a suitcase between moments of absolute happiness on stage with his accomplices and his public. Once the concerts were over, he would try to prolong that happiness by going to a bar or nightclub where he could grab something to eat, have a drink, and jam or talk with any fellow musicians he might meet there. Then he would find himself plunged back into the sombre loneliness of yet another anonymous hotel room, yet another departure, for yet another destination. The meetings he had along the way were rarely much more than brief encounters, for one night only. There was never time enough for more than a chat, a couple of beers and a memory of a friendship that might have been. But for Rory, this was the price he had to pay to realise his dream, his ultimate goal of simply becoming a better and better musician, not for the benefit of others, but for himself. As time went by, however, his endless striving for such unattainable perfection started to take its toll. He sacrificed everything in pursuit of the impossible.

From the moment when, at the age of fourteen, he had bought

his first guitar, Rory had ceased to have a private life. In the beginning he saved all the money he would have spent on going out and having fun to pay off his guitar; he never even had enough left over to take any girlfriend he might have to the cinema, and in any case, all his time was taken up with music. From that early age, he had started to create a protective shell in order to shield himself from any distractions. He had always stayed on the sidelines, with no social life whatsoever, and had consequently not had either the need or the opportunity to develop any social graces. When he was living in London, it was not rare for Gerry to go three weeks without any news of Rory.

Not until he was around thirty years old did Rory start to wonder if something was amiss. Around him, he saw his brother happily married, with a house and four children; he was godfather to all of them. He was tied down in a way, certainly, but that didn't stop him seeing his friends, going out, inviting musicians to his house: in short, living a normal life. The realisation that he might be missing out on something started to trouble him; deep down, he felt a little jealous of what others had, of what he could not have. It hurt him to know that what he wanted from his music was somehow incompatible with what he was starting to want from life. He felt he would inevitably be forced to choose between one or the other, and for him music was not a job or a career: it was a vocation, a way of life – almost like a religion, only lonelier. Rory saw it not as a problem of finding a wife, but of protecting himself from all the women who tried to take him away from his music. To Donal's great regret, the nephews and nieces that he would have liked to have were not to materialise.

Success and superstardom were not what Rory was looking for. He had no interest in having lots of money, fast cars and women buzzing round him all the time. Such superficiality did not attract him in the slightest; he was far more interested in improving his music and in producing an album that might one day go to number one in America. He was a ship without a port, with no moorings, nowhere to tie up to weather the storms of life, until one evening when he was out on the town in Chelsea with Billy Gaff, who had managed Rod Stewart and John Cougar Mellencamp, amongst others. He had also represented Rory in America. Billy told him that his flat was up for sale, a flat that had been lived in by musicians such as Elton John and Dusty Springfield. Donal told Rory that it was an excellent opportunity finally to have somewhere to call his own for a while, and Rory let himself be talked into buying the flat. He stored all his books

*Some of Rory's book collection*

about the blues, Celtic history, Ireland, James Dean, Dylan, rock music, Elvis, cinema and his detective novels there, along with his records. He put his two framed engravings of Presley – one from the 1950s, the other from the 1970s – side by side on the wall, with the ticket he had kept from the concert he'd been to in 1976 slipped into the corner of one of them, and moved in, but he never settled down.

He was a James Dean fan, appreciating the person and also the myth. He listened delightedly to Noeghan's tales of his trip to Fairmount, where Dean had grown up, and where he is buried. Noeghan told him about how he had met Ortense and Marcus Winslow, Dean's aunt and uncle, who had raised him. Rory later stuck up a poster of Dean, in jeans, bare-chested, a Texan hat on his head, and surrounded by death masks. Donal commented on how Rory loved the poster, and its morbid side, almost as if he was already becoming familiar with death. Donal gave Noeghan the poster, a present from Rory. Written on the edge was a quotation: '"Immortality is the only true success" James Dean, 1931–1955'.

Rory moved out of the flat two years before he died, and into the Conrad Hotel in Chelsea, room number 710. To get the reception to put you through to his room you had to give a code name, 'Alain

Delon', one of Rory's favourite film stars. Rory did not feel at home in England, and wanted to move to France.

# HERMAN

Herman was a Flemish cycling fan from that same strip of land between the sea and the flat country as Noeghan, Roland and the grandfather of Bob Geldof, former singer with the Boomtown Rats. Geldof was an admirer of Rory and was the organiser of the 'Band Aid' concerts in Wembley and Los Angeles, which were broadcast live and uninterrupted by almost every country in the world, except France. Due to his links with this windswept part of Europe, Geldof was made an honorary citizen of the town of Ypres. Herman Schurmans was also an honour to his country. As the former public-relations officer of an international record label, he was the founder of the Torhout and Werchter Festivals, which take place a day apart and feature the same line-up. These have been two of the most popular festivals in Europe for the last fifteen years. Professionalism, rigour, passion, love and respect made Schurmans a legend in the rock world, and a sincere friend of Rory. In July 1979, the latter had been top of the bill at one of his first festivals – a fact that Herman never forgot. Every time Rory was playing in Belgium, Herman would never fail to go along. Each year, when the festival season was over, he would devote himself to his other passion, cycling, and organise the Torhout–Werchter cycle race.

In his dressing-room in a caravan in Torhout, a large object sticking out of Noeghan's jacket pocket intrigued Rory. It was one of the first 'eurosignals ' in use, a direct between link the reporter on location and the editorial office back at the radio station. Rory found the concept amusing.

# STAGE STRUCK

The white spot on the horizon slowly redefined itself into the solid, distinguishable mass of a light aircraft, which came in to land accompanied by the deafening roar of its engines. Under a radiant sun, Rory, Gerry, Ted and Donal, the only passengers on the private flight, stepped out onto the tarmac on their way to Le Touquet in northern France, to be met by Noeghan, his wife and two daughters.

Albert Warin had a rental car waiting to follow them to the Westminster Hotel, where they were all staying. Rory was nearing the end of his third world tour, to accompany the release of the third live album, *Stage Struck,* a faithful reproduction of the energy and power that the group gave off in concert. The album featured tracks recorded in Ireland, France, Britain, the United States and Australia, from the albums *Against the Grain* ('Bought and Sold'), *Photo Finish* ('Shin Kicker', 'Brute Force and Ignorance', 'Shadow Play' and 'The Last of the Independents'), *Calling Card* ('Moonchild') and *Top Priority* ('Wayward Child' and 'Follow Me'). The remastered CD has two bonus tracks, 'Key Chain' and 'Bad Penny'.

Rory's Montreuil sur Mer concert was to be an open-air one, in the grounds of the Citadel, part of the government-financed Festival de la Côte d'Opale. France was in the throes of a national electoral campaign and the billstickers of the different parties involved were waging a veritable war with each other – a constant circular ballet of sticking, unsticking, resticking and so on. Alongside these professionals of the political poster, the festival billstickers were to be seen in action, covering every available surface with pictures of Rory. As the date of the concert approached, they were at it day and night, not motivated by the small remuneration handed out by the festival organisers, but rather by admiration for Rory. Their efforts paid off handsomely, because the concert was a sell-out, with thousands packed into the grounds, and a live radio transmission by Noeghan for Frequency Nord, the largest regional Radio France station.

The lucky few allowed backstage after the concert found Rory in high spirits, willing to talk to anyone who would listen, and they all did, marvelling at the concert they had just witnessed. After a while,

*Private flight to Le Touquet, 1981*

144

when Rory was ready to leave, Albert Warin took him to a restaurant in the old part of town, which had once been a staging post, frequented in the past by Victor Hugo and Brigitte Bardot, amongst others. The billsticking fans had followed the movement, and as Rory sat down to eat they were still standing a little way off, talking. When Noeghan explained to him that they had worked throughout the night on his behalf, Rory was touched and waved them over to sit with him at his table. The four lads were overjoyed but nonetheless cast a hesitating, questioning glance at the organiser of the Côte d'Opale festival, who returned their look with one that clearly read, 'Don't even think about it, get lost!' Disappointedly, the four felt obliged to decline Rory's offer, but he could not understand why. The festival official's attitude shocked Noeghan even more so when, at the end of the meal, the same man whispered in Warin's ear that he should pay for the meal and ask for a reimbursement later. Noeghan was ashamed to admit to Rory the real reason why the four fans had refused his offer. Warin is still waiting to be repaid for the meal.

## JINXED

Ted McKenna threw in his drumsticks and Rory had to start the arduous task of finding a replacement. The last person to audition was from Belfast and was already known to Rory as Gerry's friend and one-time drummer in Gerry's very first group, when the pair were only fourteen years old. During the 1970s, Brendan O'Neill had played in various rhythm-and-blues formations but he was also strongly influenced by jazz musicians like Miles Davies, as well as by drummers such as Tony Williams and Elvin Jones. Meanwhile, he had moved to London, had kept in touch with Gerry and had met up with Rory several times. He had heard that Rory was looking for a new drummer and had gone along to the auditions without a moment's hesitation. Over the years, his style had evolved towards rock, which suited Rory perfectly. The decision was taken, and the trio set off for Cologne to shut themselves away in the Dierks Studios, where they cut the album *Jinxed,* released in May 1982.

The trio was accompanied on the album by two other musicians, saxophonist Dick Parry (who had played on Pink Floyd's *Dark Side of the Moon*) and keyboard player Bob Andrews. *Jinxed* was essentially a rock album that gave free rein to Rory. The opening shot is the track 'Big Guns', a heavy-duty, explosive number. 'Bourbon' features a sparkling final solo, while 'Double Vision', 'Hellcat' and 'Jinxed' are dominated by weighty guitar playing prodigiously underpinned by an impeccable rhythm section. 'The Devil Made Me Do It' is a classic rock track less than three minutes long, with echoes of Buddy Holly's guitar sound. 'Ride On, Red On' is the only track that was not written by Rory himself, a homage to the little-known bluesman Louisiana Red. On one track, 'Loose Talk', Rory even plays the sitar. The remastered CD presents two bonus tracks: 'Nothin' But the Devil', featuring Rory at his best on his 1932 National, and 'Lonely Mile', dedicated to a section of the Fulham Road that Rory would walk during bouts of insomnia.

# MARK

The Bridge House Club was a well-regarded club where Nine Below Zero, a blues band, played regularly. The harmonica player was an Englishman, Mark Feltham, who had a passion for the country music of Charlie McCoy, amongst others. Throughout the 1970s, he had recorded frequently for the Monument label in Nashville and had written film scores for both television and the cinema. He had also played a lot of blues and country blues, finally forming the group Nine Below Zero with Dennis Greaves, and was a friend of Gerry's. When the group split in 1982, Gerry invited him to meet Rory, and a high level of mutual esteem quickly developed between the two men. In 1984, Donal asked him along to Pistoia in Italy to a concert in honour of Alexis Korner, who was the pioneer of British blues and a major influence for practically every musician to come out of the 1960s. Korner produced the very first radio recording of Rory for the BBC in 1968. Other participants included Jimmy Page and Ginger Baker. From that moment on, Mark was to become a permanent guest on many of Rory's recordings and would also be one of his most faithful companions, staying with him right to the very end.

The group tirelessly continued to criss-cross the world, playing on stages in many countries. Roland and Noeghan caught up with them again at the Palais des Sports in Lille, where they discovered the remarkable definition that Mark's playing added to Rory's music. Marks's playing was spontaneous and Rory, recognising this, trusted him, almost like a brother, with the freedom to improvise at will. At the Lille concert, the happiest man in the hall was the guitarist for the support act, Christophe, who had created his group, Stocks, precisely because he had for a long time been haunted and obsessed by Rory's guitar playing. Such had been the violence of emotions that he had experienced on hearing Rory's music that he had felt compelled to go out and buy a guitar, to learn how to pay it and to practise for hours on end in an effort to imitate his hero and set up his own group. His passion and insistence had culminated in the two albums and a sell-out tour of the United States. But all of this now paled into insignificance as that evening he sat in the same dressing-room as Rory, getting ready to share the same stage as him. Christophe was just one of the many musicians who have been touched and profoundly moved by Rory's music over the years. Guitarists as varied as Kurt Cobain, Slash, Johnny Marr and John Squire freely admit having been influenced by Rory; artists such as U2, Thin Lizzy, Gary Moore and Bob Geldof have all said they owe a great deal to him. But more important still, perhaps, is the effect his music has had on each of the anonymous spectators whose heart has raced on hearing Rory play: the unconditional fans, from butcher to baker, who have followed the evolution of his career as their own lives unrolled before them. Today, new groups are still forming, all over the world, from Canada to Germany, from the Netherlands to Ireland. They adopt the titles of Rory's songs as names for their bands, such as Brute Force and Ignorance, Fresh Evidence, Jinx, Blueprint, Bad Penny, the Loop, even Dave McHugh's After Taste. They pay homage to Rory and keep his music alive. Jed Thomas, Julian Sas, Caster Boire, Samuel Eddy, Martin Hutchinson, Paul Fenton and many more feel that playing for Rory is an honour in itself.

'Marie is over there!' shouted a friend of Noeghan's who was standing beside him in the concert hall. Noeghan had lost touch Marie 'Vin Blanc' (the nickname had been given to this ever-faithful fan of Rory's because she would drink only one glass of white wine) but when Rory was playing in Lille, Marie was bound to turn up. That evening, to reward her for her unyielding support for Rory, Noeghan decided to invite her backstage into the musician's dressing-room for a photo and a meeting which, he knew,

*Marie, faithful fan, and Rory, Lille 1986*

would remain forever a cherished and indelible memory for this most faithful of fans.

## STUDIO

Playing live was increasingly taking over from Rory's studio work, for it was on stage that he felt most free. Rory was a perfectionist when it came to recording, paying meticulous attention to every detail. His work-rate was enormous, with daily sessions lasting from midday to six in the morning, and his health suffered as a consequence. As soon as he woke in the morning, the first thing he did before even having breakfast was to listen over and over again to the takes of the previous day – sometimes up to twenty for a single track – between which only he was capable of distinguishing the minute differences. As a result, new album releases got gradually less frequent as he took longer and longer to be satisfied with the finished product. Sometimes he would go back over songs that had been recorded up to a year before and, as his sensibilities had changed in between times, he would no longer be happy with them, and would change studios and start again from scratch.

As Gerry remembers, for 'Rory Gallagher' and 'Deuce', the recording lasted all day, from 9 am to 7 pm, 'like a day in the BBC. We left, and the album was released. It was spontaneous, easy and free.' As time went by, they spent more and more time in the studio, sometimes staying there through the night. At times this was worthwhile; other times it was a waste of time. They would occasionally add aggression or emotions that one would not normally feel first thing in the morning. The album was polished and well-finished, but the sessions became longer and more tiring. An album would require two, even three months, and each track would be redone fourteen or fifteen times. Although this was exhausting, it was a price they chose to pay.

Rory sometimes preferred to record the first take as if he were on stage. Donal, worried, came up with the idea of setting up his own studio, so that he would feel freer to do as he wished, but Rory rejected the idea, saying that he didn't want to tie himself down to one particular place, preferring to go where the urge and the inspiration took him. Donal's next suggestion was a mobile studio, reminding Rory that he had enjoyed the recording he had been able to do in Ireland in Ronnie Lane's mobile unit. As luck would have it, Bill

Wyman, a friend of Rory and the bassist of the Rolling Stones, had the Stones' mobile studio up for sale. Donal suggested buying it, but again Rory deliberated, with the pretext that they had nowhere to store it, which was not true, as Donal had already sorted out a permanent parking lot for it when it was not in use. The truth was that Rory did not like the idea of a permanent attachment to any studio, in just the same way as he resisted any attempts to persuade him to establish a permanent home somewhere. During what were to be his last recording sessions he was often to be found in the bar drinking with the technicians and studio staff. Rory was already well on the road to serious depression.

# EXTRA

Rory always enjoyed making appearances on albums recorded by other artists, such as Albert King, Muddy Waters and Jerry Lee Lewis. During the years that separated *Jinxed* (1982) and *Defender* (1987), such guest appearances multiplied, numbering up to a dozen or more over a ten-year period. In 1984 he played on two albums with the group Box of Frogs, which was made up of three former members of the Yardbirds: Jim McCarthy on drums, Chris Dreja on rhythm guitar and Paul Samwell-Smith, the bass player and a producer for artists such as Cat Stevens. Rory worked with various artists, including Jimmy Page (also ex-Yardbirds, as were Eric Clapton and Jeff Beck) and Steve Hackett, ex-Genesis. Graham Parker, Ian Dury and Roger Chapman did the vocals. Roger Chapman and Rory gave amazing performances on *Heart and Soul*, a Yardbirds classic written by Graham Gouldman (composer of hits such as *For Your Love* and the Ten CC mega-hit *I'm Not in Love*), who also contributed to the album *Strange Land*, the second in the series.

Other collaborations included *The Scattering* for the Fureys and Davey Arthur (1989), *Out of the Air* by the Davy Spillane Band (1989), *Words and Music* with Phil Coulter (1989), *Thirty Years A-Greying* with the Dubliners (1992), *The Outstanding Album* by Chris Barber and Band (1993), *Strangers on the Run* with Samuel Eddy (1995), and a notable contribution to *A Tribute to Peter Green*, in volume 1 of *The Peter Green Songbook*. Two of these latter tracks were entitled 'Showbiz Blues' and 'Leaving Town Blues', which were strangely portentous of what was to follow.

# DEFENDER

When the contract linking him to Chrysalis came to an end with the release of *Jinx* (with a separate US release on Mercury Records), Rory decided to set up his own independent label. 'So what about a name, then?' asked Donal. After a moment's thought, Rory came up with 'Capo', for the capo on a guitar and also the head of the Mafia. So it was that Capo Records came to carry a name that could originally have referred to Al Capone! Nonetheless, Capo at last gave Rory the total artistic freedom that he had craved. He could now produce the music that *he* wanted to, without following the dictates of 'fashion'. He moved on in his own way at his own pace, and as time went by his music became increasingly 'hard', as he was hardened by life. *Defender* was a combat album – his own combat – and was sublime insomuch as he was no longer forced to make any concessions. The musicians around him – Gerry, Brendan and Mark, backed up on occasion by Lou Martin and John Cooke – were in perfect harmony with him. *Defender* went straight to the top of the Independent Charts in Britain and was charted throughout the world.

*Kickback City* expresses Rory's absolute refusal to make concessions with his music. 'Loanshark Blues' was inspired by the film *On the Waterfront,* in which a loner, played by Marlon Brando, revolts against a society built on corruption. 'Smear Campaign' denounces corruption, political sleaze and wheeler-dealing. 'Failsafe Day' carries a heartfelt anti-nuclear message. On 'I Ain't No Saint', Rory really lets himself go. 'Doing Time', which is equally intimate, paints a sound-picture of the type of anti-hero that Rory felt himself to be – the sort of person who would steal a car and smash it into a wall. 'Road to Hell' and 'Seems to Me' are simply fantastic in their thumping, rhythmic quality. 'No Peace for the Wicked' is more bluesy, thanks to his use of the 'bottle neck'. 'Seven Days' is a more acoustic number whose title was taken from one of the detective stories that Rory avidly consumed. 'Continental Op' is a straight tribute to one of Rory's favourite authors in the genre, Dashiell Hammett, who admirably depicts the shady underworld inhabited by his anti-heroes of the 1930s – the world of the backstreet blues joints or 'barrel house'. 'Don't Start Me to Talking' is in the same vein: a tribute to the bluesman Sonny Boy Williamson, author of the song, which gives ample room for Mark 'Harmonica' Feltham to let rip.

# FAIR TRADE

Catherine, Roland, Noeghan, Herman and the others were tending to go their separate ways in life, only seeing each other on odd occasions, but as soon as Rory appeared in France or Belgium, they could be sure to meet up at his side. In 1989, Rory was to play in Deinze. In his dressing-room amidst the habitual reunion festivities, Noeghan introduced Rory to a friend of his called Ludivine. Rory was rather taken by the jacket she happened to be wearing, a sort of dark-coloured windbreaker. Asking her what it was made of, he touched it lightly with his fingertips to feel the material. At this, Ludivine took it off and offered it to Rory, who was astounded. She insisted and he finally accepted, trying it on straightaway. Amazingly, it was a perfect fit. He tried to give her something for it, but she wouldn't hear of it. In his embarrassment, he opened up his suitcase, rifled through his clothes and pulled out a faded, blue denim shirt and handed it to her, thanking her profusely.

It was to be the last concert that Noeghan would see with Gerry and Brendan, who presented him with his drumsticks as he came off stage after the show. There were no backstage drinks and everyone went straight back to the hotel and shut themselves away in their respective rooms. They were running on a strict timetable the next morning. The pressure was starting to show. Rory had visibly put on weight and was thought to be suffering from something, but the subject was never brought up in public, out of decency and respect. Nothing in his attitude seemed to have changed – he was still his same old polite, kind self. Before leaving, Rory invited Noeghan to London in the run-up to Christmas: 'We're having a get-together, why don't you join us?' Noeghan never got the chance to reply.

*In the 1980s, Rory puts on weight, due to water-retention and the side-effects of prescribed medicine*

*Tickets from concerts attended by George Piat, a fan from Lille*

# JACK BRUCE

A frequent visitor to many of the world's stages, Rory had even managed to get the group behind the Iron Curtain before the fall of the Berlin Wall, where they had played in Hungary, Yugoslavia and other Eastern Bloc countries. On the way back, they stopped off in Germany, where they were extremely popular. They would play all the festivals they could, sometimes bringing in a saxophone to reinforce the impact of numbers like 'Nadine'. Festivals were a good place to meet other musicians. Frankie Miller sat in on a jam session with them, in Wiesbaden, Germany, in 1979, as did Eric Burdon in Loreley in 1982.

During a concert in Cologne on 17 October 1990, Rory came off stage after his final encore, his shirt soaked with sweat. But the houselights didn't come on. To thunderous applause, he reappeared on stage, in a black T-shirt, his guitar slung over his shoulder. He moved up to the mike. Geraint Watkins, on accordion and keyboards, took his place at the piano. Brendan climbed up on his stool, and Mark wasn't far behind. Rory turned towards the wings and announced, 'Mr Jack Bruce!' He arrived on stage, with shoulder-length hair, a mustard-yellow suit and a bass guitar swinging at his waist. He nodded to Rory, exchanged a few words, and they were off, playing 'Born Under a Bad Sign'. Bruce sang with conviction, his bass held high. Rory held himself at a distance, discreetly behind his guest. The magical voice of Cream lived again, as his fingers flew. Rory, in his turn, played 'I'm Ready'. It was fantastic rock, all held together by Brendan's keyboard interjections, and frequent exchanges between Mark and Jack.

Suddenly, Bruce launched into a solo, and it turned to jazz, before another great hit, 'Politician'. Bruce would provoke Rory, who would reply with dazzling speed, and vice versa. In sweat and laughter, they stared at each other, as if in a duel. What a duo. Their complicity was evident, and they were more than delighted to play alongside each other. The two brothers in arms often met up and even had a project lined up, to bring together other musicians of their ilk, including Belfast's Van Morrison, Charlie Watts and Ian Stewart.

# Van Morrison

Van had been in London and had not actually met Rory, but was well aware of his reputation. They first met up after a Van Morrison gig at the Rainbow, during a reception after the show to which Rory had been invited. Unfortunately, on that occasion, Van had not been in the best of moods and the two men had hardly spoken to each other all night. As Van was discreetly slipping away from the party in his car, however, he heard a man knock on the window. It was Rory, who had followed him out. Through the open window of the car, Rory introduced himself: 'Hi, I'm Rory Gallagher.' 'Yes, of course,' replied Van. 'I've heard of you, we'll have to work together sometime'.

On another occasion, Rory was playing in San Francisco, Donal had noticed that Van Morrison was on the guest list and, seeing him arrive early, had made a point of talking to him. They discovered that they had a number of mutual friends back in Northern Ireland.

Rory was headlining the Reading Festival. Harvey Goldsmith, Van's manager, contacted Donal for Van to meet Rory. Van appeared nervous and Donal found himself having to reassure the musician, but his nervous state prevented the inevitable from happening: the meeting of the two great Irishmen jamming on stage. Following the gig, Rory was invited to join Van at Manor Studios in Oxford, where the latter was recording at that time. Excited by the opportunity, Rory cancelled two dates and set off to see him. Arriving in the studio, Rory asked Van, 'So, what would you like me to play?'

Van proceeded to put on a tape of his album, whereupon he disappeared. Rory waited for him to come back – until 6 am the following morning. Rory, left alone with the American musician Dr John, was insulted by this behaviour and, collecting up his things, vowed never to work with the man again. It was then that fate took a hand in things. Catherine was visiting London, staying at Donal's house. One day the doorbell rang. Donal went to answer it, only to find himself face to face with Van Morrison.

'What are you doing here?' asked Van, puzzled,

'I live here,' replied Donal, surprised. 'I should ask you the same question.'

'I'm here to see Catherine. This is the address she gave me.'

Donal invited him in and he stayed for dinner. The evening went well and, before leaving, Van told Donal, 'I'd really like to meet Rory again.'

Donal immediately took up the opening and suggested, 'Sunday next we're having a family get-together. Why don't you come along and make the most of the opportunity to meet Rory.'

Which is precisely what he did. The two men chatted for a good while, exchanging ideas and listening to records. Nearby was a small club called the 606, where they were in the habit of going for the odd jam session. Donal had discovered this club under rather strange circumstance. On moving into his home in Fulham, he sent Roland his new address, telling him that the street on which he lived was surely one of London's smallest. Roland, in all seriousness, replied that he knew it well. He explained to the astonished Donal that there was a jazz club he knew right beside there: the 606, where he had played. Donal had no idea of the club's existence. One night, he strolled down to the club and knocked on the door. He explained that he lived nearby, to which the club-owner worriedly asked if he had come to complain about the noise. Donal reassured him, telling him he worked in the trade and that he had heard about the club. Contact had been made, and the club became one of their regular haunts. Later Donal became associate producer of BBC 2's 'Jazz 606' television series.

One day, in this club, Van declared, 'I'd like to make a blues album with Rory. I don't care what label it's on – all I care about is doing it.'

Rory was in Scotland at that time, working with Jack Bruce for a blues-concert collaboration, with Charlie Watts on drums and Ian Stewart on keyboards, and Rory and Jack on guitars and vocals, along with a brass section. It was during this collaboration that Donal had been approached to make a music programme based on a blues session by Rory for the RTÉ series *The Sessions* and he suggested that this would be the ideal line-up and location for all parties involved. The programme brought together musicians from different horizons, such as the Dubliners and the Pogues, for a sessions-type show. It seemed the ideal opportunity to get the Morrison–Gallagher project off the ground, with the added bonus of a ready-made live album into the bargain. A date was fixed for the broadcast, and a number of meetings took place, but Van was still a little reticent. 'It's great,' he said, 'but I know next to nothing about the blues', to which Rory replied, 'Hang on, you're one of the main people responsible for popularising traditional blues in this country!' Finally, just two weeks before the broadcast, Van Morrison, who as always was extremely busy, abandoned the project – much to Rory's regret. Rory, who was now starting to feel nervous about things himself, gave way to his request and the project was dropped. Later, Van also regretted his decision.

*(Left to right) Jean-Noël Coghe, Rory and Roland in Louvain*

*(Left to right) Catherine, Rory and Roland in Deinze, 1990*

*(Left to right) Leslie, Rory and Roland*

# FRESH EVIDENCE

As with the *Defender* album, Rory's new recording project involved sessions in several different studios, including Kedan. He took with him the usual line-up of Gerry McAvoy, Brendan O'Neill and Mark Feltham, plus John Cooke and Lou Martin on keyboards, and a brass section made up of John Earle on tenor and baritone sax, Ray Beavis on tenor and Dick Hanson on trumpet. This album, which was to be his last, went back over all of Rory's favourite music styles – blues, rock and jazz – in a number of his own compositions.

'Kid Gloves', an energetic rock number, makes references to the John Huston film *Fat City*. 'The King of Zideco' pays tribute to Clifton Chenier and his Cajun music, whence the need for the accordion, which also features on 'Never Asked You for Nothing', another track that takes no prisoners. 'Middle Name' is another tribute, this time to John Lee Hooker and the America that Rory loved. 'Alexis' is an instrumental dedicated to Alexis Korner, the father of British blues, and is also influenced by Rory's beloved jazz. Another instrumental, 'The Loop', takes its name from the public-transport system in Chicago. 'Empire State Express', featuring his Dobro (National Duolin 1932), is a further homage to the Delta blues and one of its foremost components, Eddie 'Son' House, who was much admired by Rory. The guitar playing on this particular track is spellbinding. The sparkling introduction to 'Ghost Blues' is part-Celtic, part-blues, played first on the sitar, and then electrified, with Gerry and Brendan setting off at a frenetic pace, punctuated by Mark's incisive harmonica. 'Heaven's Gate' is another stunning track. 'Walkin' Wounded' is in the same spirit, with Rory, on top of an insistent beat, giving vent to that sense of unease that often invaded him. 'Slumming Angel' is pure rock and Rory! In 'Bowed Not Broken', Rory gives us another glimpse of his inner self, and this makes the track even more touching.

# BREAK UP

He had not taken the decision lightly, but prior to the last, four-month-long world tour, culminating in a concert in New York, Gerry and Brendan announced to Rory that they were leaving the group. Gerry had for a while been nurturing his own projects and writing his own music; now he wanted to develop his own career. The decision hurt and saddened him greatly, but after twenty years spent faithfully at Rory's side, he felt it was something he just had to do. It was the end of an alchemy between the two guitarists that could never be replaced. Brendan, who himself had been with Rory for ten years, decided to follow Gerry, and the two of them teamed up with Dennis Greaves, the founder member of Nine Below Zero (Mark's former group), to raise the band once more from its ashes. Rory dutifully set about the task of finding new musicians with whom to get back on stage in order to exorcise his angst. They were later to meet on stage, sharing the same line-up: Gerry and Brendan playing support with Nine Below Zero, at the Bonn Blues festival in December 1993.

Rory had for some time admired Jeff Beck's drummer Tony Newman, who had been a session musician in Nashville for artists like the Everly Brothers and Dolly Parton. His son, Richard, had taken over the reins from his father, playing with the likes of Steve Marriott, and it was Richard who was to replace Brendan O'Neill. Jim Leverton, the keyboard player, was also an accomplished bassist, having accompanied Noël Reading in the group Fat Mattress, as well as Steve Marriott in the Packet of Three. Rory had previously met him when Fat Mattress were on tour with Taste. Jim was with them on several tours. Mark Feltham remained as harmonica player. On the *Defender* album the bass was played by David Levy, whose style was different from, and more supple than, Gerry's. So Rory once again found himself surrounded by a collection of exceptional musicians to support him not only musically, on stage, but also morally, in the ups and downs of everyday life.

# RORY ON STAGE

Leslie was lucky, tucked up all warm and cosy in her mother's womb. She was at dinner at her parents' house with Peter Hammill. When she was born, in July 1977, Rory Gallagher sent her a telegram welcoming her into the world! When she was three months old, Maxime Le Forestier cradled her in his arms. But at sixteen she was Cure-d! She only had eyes for Robert Smith.

One day, Noeghan got a phone call from Roland: 'He's playing in Ghent on Saturday. He seems to be a lot better, and he's back on tour, finishing with Ghent.' So the rendezvous was set. Noeghan decided to take his daughter, Leslie, along with him to the mythical venue the Vooruit, which was situated in a Ghent cul-de-sac and was covered with graffiti, making it look like something out of 1960s London. 'It's crawling with Apaches!' remarked Leslie as they walked past dozens of middle-aged men in jeans, boots and leather jackets. Rory arrived, wearing an old raincoat, just before the concert was due to start, and Noeghan introduced him to Leslie, whom he had not seen for ten years. After giving her a big hug, he looked her in the eyes and told her, 'Your father is a good friend of mine, you know.' Throughout the evening, his behaviour seemed strange to Roland, Herman, Mao from Lille, and the people from Holland and elsewhere who knew him and were gathered there for the occasion. Someone produced a camera, and Rory, Roland and Leslie obligingly posed for the photo, whereupon Rory suddenly put his hand on Leslie's shoulder and, with a strangely intense look in his eyes, said to her, 'Look after your father's health, won't you. Health is a very precious thing.'

At the start of the concert, Noeghan took his daughter into the audience, where they found Catherine. The concert was very long that night, lasting over two and a half hours – a little too long for the adolescent Cure fan's tastes, who towards the end was starting to get impatient, complaining about 'all these bloody Apaches!' On stage, Rory suddenly produced an acidic guitar riff and took hold of the mike and declared, in front of 1,500 people, 'It's good to back in Ghent. Special thanks to Catherine, to Roland and to Noeghan', before setting off into a violent, screaming solo. Leslie turned to her father and demanded, 'Are you happy now?' Yes, he was happy – ecstatic even, and very, very proud. Catherine squeezed his hand to get his attention and whispered in his ear, 'What's going on, do you think? Something's up with Rory.' Backstage, a lot of well-wishers and friends were milling around Rory, who had put his raincoat back on and was talking, laughing, signing autographs and posing for photos. One person had even brought a guitar for him to sign, which he was delighted to do. A nearby restaurant had been requisitioned. Rory insisted that Catherine and Leslie sit on each side of him; he ate very little and spent most of the meal talking to Leslie, who, at sixteen, had to admit she was having a little trouble understanding his Irish accent!

At the end of the meal, there was noticeable tension between Rory and his brother, Donal, but whatever it was, it ended quickly with a shrug of Donal's shoulders. Mark then led Donal out of the restaurant, and most of the other musicians followed suit. Jim stayed

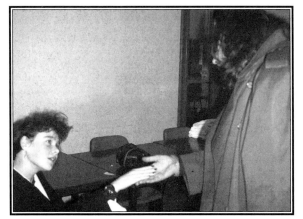

*Leslie and Rory*

*Rory and Mao*

*Leslie, Catherine and Rory in Ghent, 1992*

*Rory signs a Fender guitar, Ghent, 1992*

with Rory, who suggested moving on to one of the typical Belgian bars with which Ghent is particularly well blessed. The beer and music started flowing, and Rory sat down at a table a little apart from the others to talk to Catherine, intensely, for what seemed like hours. Respecting their intimacy, and sensing the intensity of the discussion, Roland, Noeghan, Jim, Leslie and Mao stayed at the bar until about 6 am, when Noeghan announced that it was time he got Leslie back. Rory got up and said his fond, warm-hearted farewells. 'That evening,' Catherine later told Noeghan, 'he talked to me like he'd never done before, about his innermost feelings and the things that were dearest to his heart. It was almost as if he sensed that his days were numbered.' Catherine was never again to see Rory alive.

After the tour was over, Rory set about work on a compilation album called *Edged in Blue,* released on Capo/Demon Records, having recently got back the rights to all his previous recordings. Taking his cue from Frank Zappa, he even went so far as to produce his own bootleg copies in order to outwit the pirates. Thus was born a three-CD box set entitled *G-Men* (another B-movie reference!), which brought together live recordings from all over the world and featured most of the musicians Rory had ever played with. The album therefore included some extraordinary spontaneous passages by gifted artists playing completely free from the pressures and constraints of the organised, programmed, official live takes. Despite its inevitable raw, warts-and-all character, it includes some incredible improvisations, such as the stunning versions of *Cradle Rock* and *Bullfrog Blues.*

This was one of many projects Rory was involved in at the time. He also wanted to do an acoustic album with one side of pure blues and a B-side dedicated to folk music inspired by traditional Irish or

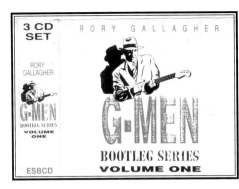

Celtic roots. 'If God can spare me the time,' he is noted as having said, 'I'd like to do one more electric and one more acoustic album – a double album. Why not?'

At the end of October 1994 (after the date of the gig was changed), Noeghan, in his capacity as a journalist, had been camped out for several days

*Collector's box containing the three 'official' bootleg recordings of Rory Gallagher*

in front of a high school in Lille that was teeming with police, other journalists, onlookers and parents. The affair of the 'tchador', or Muslim headscarf, was at its height. Girls from the school refused to remove this symbol of their religion in class; the French state education system, however, prohibits any outward indication of religious creed. Both sides were guilty of manipulative tactics but it was the girls themselves who were suffering the consequences and exclusions. Noeghan had more than one reason for wishing that some sort of compromise be reached very rapidly. It was after ten in the evening, and Rory's concert at the Aeronef, the famous rock venue in Lille, had already started!

Finally, he managed to get away and rushed over to the hall, slipping in by the stage in time to witness the last three numbers. Albert Warin was already there, and he told Noeghan that Rory was really giving it his all that night. Sweating profusely, as always, he was shooting notes out in machine-gun-like bursts of tortured intensity. 'He can't be more than three metres away from me, but he's somewhere else completely,' breathed Noeghan, 'yet I feel myself transported towards him, in complete harmony with what he's expressing. As if what he's playing, at the precise moment when he plays it, is exactly what I was hoping for and expecting. In Rory's playing that night, there was a desperate, undeniable sense of force and fury. Mark Feltham never let him out of his sight for an instant, as if covering him, carrying him through a battlefield. He played *Bye, Bye Bird*. It was to be my last concert with Rory.

'Immediately after the gig, Rory came straight over to me and threw his arms around me, hugging me tight for what seemed like an eternity. This was something he had never before done. Then he

*Rory at the Aeronef, Lille, October 1994*

AW Production
présente

# RORY GALLAGHER

VENDREDI 14 OCTOBRE 1994 / 20 HEURES   130 FRANCS
L'AERONEF / LILLE

*Backstage pass for a Rory Gallagher concert in Lille, 1994. (Above) concert ticket – note the different dates: the concert had been postponed*

poured me a drink. Warin was there with his wife, Simone, and his daughter, Aurore, whom Rory had last seen as a tiny baby in Dourges. The photos taken in Ghent with Roland, who was stuck in Brussels and couldn't be at the concert, were passed around with others of my house in the south and of the Ardeche region of France, where Albert had opened a hotel. "Why don't you all come and visit me?" said Warin, and Donal took up the idea, saying that the group had been planning to record during the summer of 1995, and so why not in the south of France? "That way we can come to your house too, Noeghan," he said.'

Dinner afterwards was in the town centre. It was getting on for midnight when they arrived at the restaurant, and Donal took Noeghan aside, saying, 'Lille has changed a lot recently. I thought it might be a good idea to buy a flat for Rory here. With the tunnel, it's close

*Lille, October 1994, from left to right: Rory, Aurore and Albert Warin, Jean-Noël Coghe*

164

to London, Paris and Brussels, and he would have you and Roland around to be friends with. It would be good for Rory – a place where he could work in peace and quiet.' Noeghan was naturally charmed by the idea. 'Tell me exactly what you're looking for,' he said, 'and I'll take care of everything.'

Rory and Mark sat down next to Noeghan at the table. It was the first time Rory had had a chance to get to know the harmonica player properly. It soon became evident that Mark was devoted to him. Rory himself appeared to be in good form that evening, although once again he hardly touched what he had ordered, and was drinking very little too. He was, however, in a talkative mood, telling Noeghan all about the shopping he'd done that afternoon in the pedestrian streets of Lille. He had discovered, by chance, a shop owned by a friend of Albert Warin's, where he had bought some miniature guitars for his collection, as well as lots of other little knick-knacks that he'd found amusing. The shop owner in question, who happened to be there in the restaurant with Albert, was flattered, and at the end of the meal he asked if he might take a few photos of Rory with Albert and his daughter. Rory, of course, agreed, and dragged Noeghan into the group with him.

Finally, at around three in the morning, they all left the restaurant and headed for Rory's hotel, a few metres away on the main square. As they were walking along, Rory took Noeghan by the arm and said, 'Come and fetch me tomorrow and we'll have lunch together.' At first Noeghan refused, saying, 'Forget it, you're leaving for London tomorrow – you're better off catching up on some sleep', but Rory insisted, saying, 'I'll be waiting for you at half past twelve!'

At the arranged time the next day, Noeghan entered the Bellevue Hotel and had the receptionist phone up to Rory's room to let him know he was there. Rory appeared almost immediately with his bag ready and led Noeghan off in the direction of a nearby restaurant, La Chicorée, where Mark and David Levy were already waiting. Once again he only managed a couple of mouthfuls of the steak that he had ordered, drank a single beer and chatted about this and that: about the cinema, about the admiration he had for the French actor Lino Ventura as a man and an actor. After a while Mark and David left and the two of them were left talking, just as they had done the very first time, twenty years previously in the Rue des Bouchers in Brussels. The landlady of the restaurant, who recognised Rory from a magazine article she'd read, asked if she and her daughter could have their photo taken with him. He smiled as Noeghan took a few snaps and the landlady thanked him and signalled to the waiter to bring over a bottle of champagne to have a toast. Noeghan noticed that Rory brought the glass to his lips but discreetly avoided drinking any of the champagne, preferring to pour it into a flower-pot next to the table when the landlady had gone.

It was approaching three o'clock in the afternoon by the time Donal came in to tell them it was time to go. Rory picked up the bill and they returned to the hotel, where two cars were waiting out front, their motors running. Shaking his hand long and hard, Rory thanked Noeghan for everything and told him to take great care of himself, before getting into one of the Renault Safrannes with the others. Rory gave a final wave as the cars disappeared into the flow of traffic, leaving Noeghan alone on the pavement, deep in thought.

In the middle of December, Rory was in Ris-Orangis for what was to be an unusual concert – and one of his last on French soil. It was to take place in a club, with a capacity of only 500 people, which was run as a project designed to get long-term unemployed youngsters off the dole queue and into some professional experience. The project was celebrating ten years of existence and they had tried their luck and invited Rory along to play, aware that his legendary friend-liness and authenticity would be a good example for the young, underprivileged people involved. They never dreamt that he would accept, however. 'We can't pay much,' they had said, but for Rory this was of no importance: the concert went ahead and was extra-ordinary. The proximity to the packed audience and the intimacy of the club reminded him of the Piblokto in Dourges, where he had played his first-ever concerts in France: he felt the same passion, the same love.

At the end of December, he was back in Belgium again, with Roland at the Luna Club, and this time it was Noeghan who was unable to go. In the spring, he was booked to play at the Printemps de Bourges festival but, reading through the write-ups afterwards, Noeghan was surprised to find no mention anywhere of Rory's name – not one line! This was logical as it turned out: Rory was already in hospital, but had kept it a secret.

*December, 1994. Rory on stage at Le Plan in Ris-Orangis*

*Rory on stage at the Luna, December 1994*

# DEATH ON PRESCRIPTION

Contrary to popular belief, alcohol was not the real reason for Rory's death. Like any self-respecting Irishman, he did drink his fair share. Even Donal freely admitted to drinking, at times, more than his brother, who was in turn worried about *him!* Rory was an artist: the genuine article, gifted right across the artistic range, from painting and writing to music, blessed with a rare sensitivity that made him timid by nature but ready to give his all to his music in a constant effort to push himself to the limit and even, finally, over the edge.

In the early 1980s Rory had been consulting a doctor for a while to combat his fear of flying, anguish and stress. The doctor had been prescribing regular doses of tranquilisers, to which Rory had gradually become addicted without anyone around him realising. When he got in a plane, to calm his fear of flying he would take a pill; when he couldn't sleep, he would take a pill; when he was worried or worked up about something, or when he wanted to fight his urge to sleep when he was working, he took a pill. Rory was experiencing increasingly obvious and negative side effects. His body would swell up, he had mood swings, he got depressed, and eventually he started drinking heavily once more. That final, fatal combination pushed him over the edge. Before a concert, he would be calm and serene and then suddenly he would get stage fright, saying he couldn't go through with it.

It was in 1990 that Donal started to realise what was going on. Rory was suffering from slightly high blood pressure and went into a clinic for some tests. The doctors were categorical: Rory's body was clogged up; he was taking large quantities of some kind of a harmful substance; alcohol alone could not be the cause. They recommended he seek professional help to help him kick his habit. Rory, however, did not, and would not listen to reason. The only other solution for Donal was to keep a close eye on Rory, and the best way to do that was to go on tour, where he would be constantly surrounded by people who were close to him, and by his musicians. When he was not on the road, Rory would shut himself away at home all day and phone up at midnight saying he wanted to go for a drink or a bite to eat. He lived completely out of sync with the rest of the world. Donal couldn't possibly stay out till six in the morning and be in the office for nine. So Rory would become increasingly isolated, then lonely, then depressed; finally, he would seek refuge in his pills.

Donal had managed to persuade him to consult a different doctor to get his treatment modified, but Rory had returned to see the original one behind his back and was rapidly spiralling downwards. It was a vicious circle, with Rory drinking brandy as a stimulant and then taking anti-depressants to counteract the lows that followed once the alcohol had worn off. The situation was becoming critical. Donal tried desperately to reason with Rory, but to no avail. Finally, Donal decided to write to the doctor to explain the situation and the state of his brother's health, asking him to stop supplying the pills in question. The doctor showed the letter, which was supposed to be confidential, to Rory, who felt betrayed by his brother, and this only served to deepen his depression. In the months leading up to this, Donal had managed to limit the damage by confiscating any pills that he found. For a few weeks, in the run-up to Christmas, he succeeded in limiting his medication.

The usual rhythm in the past had been to interrupt the concerts for Christmas and to go back on the road in the spring at the start of the festival season. That year, however, Donal decided to avoid this period of inactivity, which was so detrimental to Rory, and organised a few gigs in Holland for the beginning of 1995. In the middle of January, several of the musicians came down with a bad dose of the flu, as did Rory – only in his case it was further aggravated by a bronchial infection. The truth was that Rory's liver had ceased to function correctly and his blood was not being filtered as it should; this had repercussions on his brain and he was no longer able to reason normally. He increasingly saw his brother as the enemy, preventing him from procuring the medicines that he thought he needed. Back in London, Donal, at his wits' end, could no longer contain himself. He told Rory, 'You need to get to hospital! You need help!' Rory would not listen.

This was too much for Donal, who decided deliberately to provoke his brother into reacting. 'Look, you've got three choices: an undertaker, police or an ambulance,' he said. 'You need to go to hospital straightaway and I'll drive you there myself.'

Rory hesitated, and asked for time to think it over. 'Give me until tomorrow, will you?' he asked.

'You don't have a tomorrow.'

'OK, give me just one hour.'

When Donal came back an hour later, Rory said, 'I'll go', and Donal drove him straight to the nearby Cromwell Hospital.

When Rory lapsed into a coma, he was transferred to King's

College Hospital to undergo a liver transplant operation. To this day, Donal stills wonders whether he was right to insist on trying everything at that stage, and feels somehow guilty about depriving his brother of a more natural death. At that moment, however, he had had no alternative but to seize every possible opportunity to save his brother's life. The transplant was a success and by late May the doctors were telling Donal that his brother was going to make it and that he would soon be able to leave the transplant centre at King's College Hospital to go back to Cromwell Hospital, which was close to both their homes. Two days before the transfer was due, Rory caught a virus.

The doctors didn't appear unduly worried by this new turn of events but decided nonetheless to keep him in the clinic a little while longer until he got over it. But Rory was still weak and his immune system was not able to cope; his condition got steadily worse as the virus spread. The doctors then decided to put him under general anaesthetic for a few days in order to let his body rest completely to combat the infection more effectively. Perhaps at the same time, they were already thinking that such a measure might spare him from any unnecessary suffering. Donal left Rory lying on his bed and went towards the door. Before leaving the room, he turned, to see Rory smiling faintly and giving him the thumbs-up sign. Rory died on 14 June 1995, at 10.44 am.

To brighten up his room during the three months that Rory had spent there, Donal had asked permission to hang a few posters up on the bare walls – cinema posters recalling some of Rory's favourite films – and as he took them down now, he realised that they all shared a strange, macabre connotation: *The Big Sleep, Tomorrow Never Comes* and *Heaven Can Wait*.

Throughout his stay in hospital, Rory had expressed the wish that his illness be kept secret from all but a few close friends and family, which included Mark and Tom. Out of a sense of pride, he didn't want anybody to know what was happening to him; when he got back into the limelight (because he surely thought that he would), he didn't want people constantly coming up to him and saying, 'So, are you better now?' Or was it that he wanted to be remembered as a good musician and guitarist, not because of his operation?

'When I was a Cowboy'
Western Plain

# THE FUNERAL

That evening when he got home, his younger daughter, Jennifer, told him, 'Your friend Roland phoned. He said he'd call you back later.' Noeghan made light of that: 'Of course he will. "Later" as in in three months' time, as per usual. Today's phone call is already the one he was going to give me six months ago!' Later that evening, while going through his papers, he came across some old negatives in a faded envelope. They were of the television programme with Rory in 1975. Funny, he'd forgotten they'd ever existed. A little after 8 pm, the telephone rang; his wife, Martine, picked it up. Seeing the look on her face, he guessed there was something wrong, and hurried to answer. 'It's Roland here,' said the trembling voice on the other end of the line, before falling silent for an instant. 'It's our old mate in London,' he finally went on. 'He's pulled a fast one on us all. He's done a runner, understand? He ... he ... Donal phoned me earlier to let me know and I tried to get hold of you ... He died this morning, Noeghan, in hospital. He's dead.'

By just before ten o'clock, Noeghan couldn't keep the news to himself any more. He had to tell someone, so he rang RTL, one of the major national radio stations in France. He asked to speak to Fabrice Lundy, the journalist who did the 10.15 news round-up. Fabrice puts him through to Francis Zégut, whom Noeghan had never met, but whom, from his reputation, Neoghan felt would be the right person to announce such an event, which would deeply affect all the humble, anonymous ones, who sincerely loved and respected Rory. Zégut, clearly moved by the news, called him back late that night to get more details about what had happened. Noeghan had already gone to bed but agreed to answer Zégut's questions, knowing that the other man must be able to hear that he was crying.

The AFP (the French Press Agency) announced the news officially at lunchtime the next day. 'I've sent a fax to Donal expressing our condolences,' Noeghan told his wife. 'I heard from Pascal Bernadin, who's already over there, that the funeral is fixed for Monday, in Cork, Ireland.' 'You have to go,' replied Martine, and called a travel agent's to book three tickets: one for him, one for Roland, who in the end couldn't get away, and one for Leslie, who wasn't sure if she could face it. The following Sunday, Catherine called, in tears. 'If you're going, I'm coming with you,' she said.

The night of the municipal elections, Noeghan had to work until midnight, but his mind was already elsewhere. Early the following morning, Catherine, Leslie and Noeghan set off for Roissy Airport in Paris. The flight to Cork was half-empty. At the stopover in Dublin, a man got on and sat near them. 'He's going to Rory's funeral,' whispered Catherine. 'I recognise him – it's Martin Carthy, a guitarist that Rory wanted to work with. He stayed over at Roland's one time.' When they arrived in front of the church, he was indeed present – along with 4,000 others!

It was a mild, grey, rainy day. Cork, like the weather, was in mourning, because she was about to bury one of her children. Centre stage in the vast church was a coffin covered with flowers. Until now it had always been Rory who entered once the audience was in place; this one last time he was already there, waiting for them. His family and close friends were in the first rows: his mother, Mona, sitting very dignified next to Donal; Donal's wife, Cecilia, and their four children; then Tom, Gerry and the others. Crowds of people, young and old, were filling the pews; an old woman, holding a flower, was moving her lips in silent prayer. Anonymous fans, friends and inhabitants of Cork were standing side by side with show-business celebrities: among them Gary Moore, the Dubliners, and Adam Clayton and the Edge from U2. From somewhere high up in the rafters, the cry of a violin suddenly rang out – the violionist was Matt Cranitch. At this point, Tom moved slowly towards the coffin and handed his old Fender to Rory for the last time, placing it among the flowers at the front of the church.

The whole ceremony was moving and dignified, heavy with meaning. A dog was trotting up and down the aisles, reminding Noeghan of the stray he had picked up in Brussels after one of Rory's concert; no one chased it away. Rory's nieces and nephews did the

*Rory's coffin on the way to the cemetery in Cork*

173

readings, and some of his closest friends also addressed the congregation. Then suddenly, a few notes of blues rang out as Lou Martin and Mark Feltham paid a final homage to Rory, with their rendition of 'A Million Miles Away'. Noeghan had brought with him the old Nagra that he'd taken with him on tour for the first time with Rory and discreetly he set it running, the tears streaming down his face. Finally, Tom took back the Fender as Donal, Ronnie Drew from the Dubliners, Tom and three other friends lifted the coffin onto their shoulders and advanced back down the church, passing between rows of people weeping and crossing themselves, to place it delicately in the waiting hearse.

Donal then spotted Noeghan and came over to hold him for an instant in his arms before the mass of mourners starting moving silently in the direction of the cemetery, a few kilometres outside the town, set amongst the rolling green hillsides. As Noeghan approached the cemetery, driven by someone he did not know, he could see that there were already hundreds of people grouped on the pavements, standing in silent tribute to Rory. The cars could get no closer than two kilometres from the graveyard because of the throng of people, so they abandoned the vehicles and went the rest of the way on foot, a silent procession of at least 2,000 mourners trooping towards the already besieged cemetery. A light rain was falling, and the breeze made the trees all around shiver as Rory was finally laid to rest. Prayers were said and 'Amazing Grace' floated out from Mark's harmonica at the graveside, surrounded by the family. Unsteady and breathless, he was crying as he played.

Little by little the crowd dispersed, until only one or two people remained around the grave. A young man handed Noeghan a shovel, saying, 'If you would like to ... ' Noeghan sprinkled a little earth onto the harmonica that Mark had moments before dropped onto the coffin, while a German woman, dressed in black, with long hair falling over her shoulders, stood paralysed by grief, trembling, unable to hold back her tears, unable to tear herself away.

As they were leaving, Noeghan took one last look in the direction of Rory's final resting place, and high up in the sky, regal, frozen in midflight, a seagull hung motionless, its immense wings spread wide and majestic, floating noiselessly on the air. Rending the silence with a cry, it swooped down over Rory's grave, before suddenly beating its outstretched wings, raising its head and soaring away into the infinite distance, engulfed by a cloud.

The wake afterwards was being held, quite by chance, in the

*The crowd in front of Rory's grave*

hotel where Noeghan, Leslie and Catherine were staying. Tom was waiting in the foyer to guide them into the reception room. At the door, two men were making sure no uninvited guests entered, and they started to ask Noeghan to leave his tape recorder outside, but Donal signalled to them that it was all right, and came over to talk to him. 'It's really a relief,' he said. 'After the operation on 25 March, everything seemed to be fine, but then with the complications that followed he suffered a lot. In the last days I asked Mark to stop by the hospital to play at Rory's bedside, and amazingly the heart monitor picked up a reaction. Rory could hear the music, I'm sure of it. The next day the doctors couldn't believe how relaxed and calm his expression had become. He looked a lot better.' But he hadn't been able to hold out, he was gone, but peacefully, with his head and his heart full of his music.

And so it was even on this day of mourning, in death as in life, that music once again, inevitably, took centre stage. In the corner of the room stood a piano, and Lou Martin found himself absent-mindedly moved towards it. As he started lightly caressing its keys, guitars appeared from nowhere, and Rory's friends started playing and singing for him in turn.

Nearly all had tears in their eyes, but this was Ireland, Rory's Ireland, and music was a natural part of it, impossible to resist. Gerry and the renowned Irish song-writer Jimmy McCarthy played guitar, Lou the piano, Feltham his harmonica, as the songs and other musicians followed one after another. Some were Rory's songs, or Bob Dylan's, or other classics: 'Calling Card', 'Runaway', 'Be Bop a Lula',

175

and many more. The musicians sang their praises to Rory, and Noeghan, as he had always done, recorded it all for posterity, to keep a record of what was now over.

Nothing would ever be the same again. So long, Rory, thank you, thank you for your goodness, for your sincerity, for your music, for your *soul* music. Time and rock music wait for no man.

In the corner of the room, Leslie, Noeghan's daughter, is talking to Eoin, Rory's nephew and godson. They talk for a long time, become friends. They are still writing to each other to this day.

*Brendan O'Neill, Johnny Campbell, Lou Martin*

*Gerry McAvoy, Mark Feltham, Donal*

*Gerry and Mark*

*Gerry McAvoy,
Donal Gallagher,
Jimmy McCarthy,
Mark Feltham and
a friend*

## The Cork Examiner

*Rory Gallagher's brother, Donal, and Ronnie Drew of The Dubliners shoulder the guitarist's coffin during the funeral yesterday.* (Pictures: Maurice O'Mahony)

### Stars bid farewell to Rory

By DICK BRAZIL, Special Correspondent

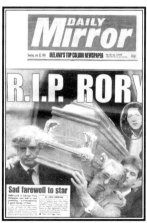

*Front page of the newspapers
the day after Rory's funeral*

# Moving On

RTL's six o'clock news presenter called Noeghan to ask him to do a short piece on the latest incident on the Shuttle: 'No more than forty seconds. Sinclair is taking up ten minutes, and afterwards I've got Maxime Le Forestier coming in.'

'Maxime?' Noeghan exclaimed. 'Do me a favour, could you – tell him from me that Rory has passed away.'

Just after six, the phone rang again; this time it was Maxime. He seemed sincerely touched by the news, as Noeghan described what had happened and told him about the funeral, mentioning in passing the dog in the church. 'Just like for Mozart,' remarked Maxime, 'minus the crowd!'

A little while later, Noeghan got a call from Albert Warin: 'Pascal Bernadin is organising some concerts for Toto. We thought your friend Roland would be perfect as the supporting act.' Coincidentally, Roland was on hold on the other line, and he agreed to do ten dates as a tribute to Rory, 'Dedicated to my old friend Rory Gallagher, St James Infirmary'.

In Ris-Orangis, a Parisian suburb, Rory was to have a street named after him, running alongside Le Plan Club, as a gesture of thanks for the concert he'd done there. The decision was passed unanimously by the town council, by members of all political persuasions. The official inauguration of the street took place in the presence of Rory's mother, Mona, Donal, Tom and several others who had been close to Rory. In the crowd, town dignitaries, representatives of the Irish embassy and faithful fans such as Little Bob, who had come all the way from Le Havre especially for the occasion, mixed with the likes of Alan Stivell, Nine Below Zero. The Irish and

*The mayor of Ris-Orangis inaugurates Rue Rory Gallagher. On the left we see Donal and Rory's mother, Mona*

French media came. His mother expressed her enormous pride in her son, and thanked the people of France, young and not so young, for turning out to share such a marvellous moment with her. In Ireland, they are planning other ways of paying homage to Rory; discussion about this are taking place in Cork. But, as the newspapers acknowledged, France had beaten them to it.

On 8 November, Catherine, Roland and Noeghan went to a memorial mass in London in memory of Rory. It was a dignified ceremony at which Bob Geldof, Van Morrison and others were also present. One surprise guest was Rory's former drummer, Rod de Ath, who, despite his long absence from the public eye following a serious accident, had insisted on coming.

At the reception afterwards in Ireland House, Van Morrison, never taking off his hat, talked for a long time with Mark Feltham. More than a hundred people were present, and their glasses were refilled as quickly as they could be emptied. Dozens and dozens of barrels of beer were drunk dry, and afterwards a select few were invited back to Donal's house to carry on the evening. Roland and Van parted on good terms towards 6 am. For Noeghan, duty called: he had to return to Lille to submit a story about the twenty-fifth anniversary of the death of General de Gaulle that he had done the previous day at Colombey-les-

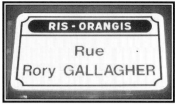

The Church Of The London Oratory
Brompton Road
London SW1

*Rory Gallagher*
March 2, 1948 - June 14, 1995

**Memorial Mass**

*Booklet and CD given to those who attended the celebration mass, 8 November 1995*

179

*London, November 1995, leaving the church after mass in memory of Rory*

*Rory's grave in Cork*

*Bronze sculpture erected in Rory Gallagher Place*

Deux-Églises, and which he still had to work up on the Eurostar so that his report could go out on the radio the next day.

Each year, the birth and death of Rory are commemorated around the world. Concerts are organised in Cork, London and Belfast. The Irish Minister of Education is on record as saying that 'The impact that Rory has had on modern Ireland is enormous!'

Another tribute to Rory – in which Hank Marvin, Jack Bruce and Peter Green, among others, participated – was put together by Fender. Several Web sites preserve his memory on the Internet. On his grave, a stunning bronze memorial headstone by Eoin Ó Riabhaigh (a musician himself), in conjunction with the National Sculpture Factory has been erected. Another sculpture in tribute to Rory, by a childhood friend of his, Geraldine Creedon, can be seen on what is now Rory Gallagher Place, in the centre of Cork city.

In Hamburg, Rory's name has been added to the plaque that commemorates the former Star Club, and every year German television broadcasts a Rockpalast concert given by Rory. Donal produced a superb double album, *BBC Sessions*, selected from its impressive stock of archive material – Rory being their most recorded artist in the last thirty years. Tom and Donal are working on, and have archived, a vast collection of documents, articles, videos and artefacts linked to Rory's career, with a view to opening a mobile exhibition dedicated to his memory.

*Jean-Noël Coghe and the guitar, London, March 1999*

*After Rory's death, the artist Mania created these three panels in homage to Rory. Using a quill, these ink drawings were published in the Le Goinfre review, October 1995*

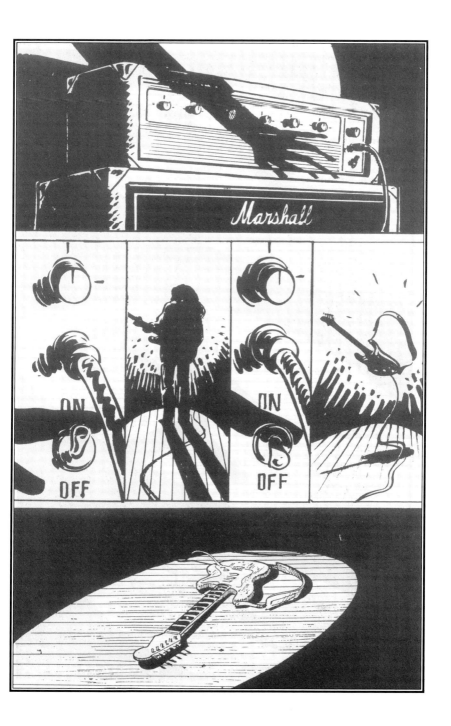

183

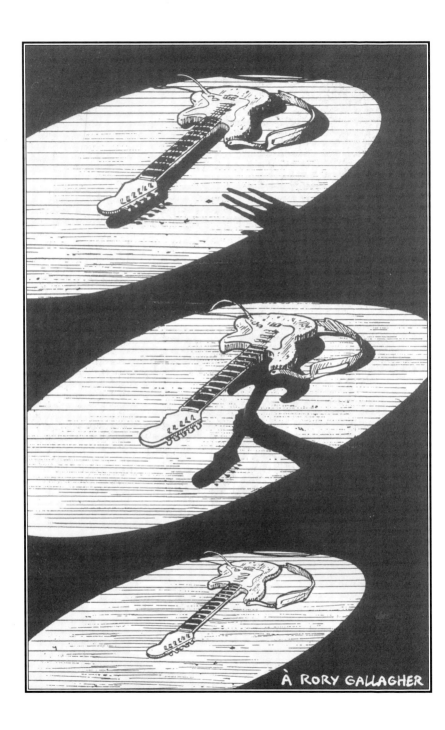

À RORY GALLAGHER

# THE KING, RORY

*Ruary*
*In the kingdom of the harp*
*King Rory made a guitar his queen*

# CDS OF RORY GALLAGHER

Capo Records. Distribution BMG/RCA
  – Rory Gallagher (May 1971) Capo 101 ref. 7432 1601012
  – Deuce (November 1971) Capo 102 ref. 7432 1601022
  – Live in Europe (May 1972) Capo 103 ref. 7432 1601032
  – Blueprint (February 1973) Capo 104 ref. 7432 1601042
  – Tattoo (November 1973) Capo 105 ref. 7432 1601052
  – Irish Tour (July 1974) Capo 106 ref. 7432 1601062
  – Against the Grain (1975) Capo 107 ref. 7432 1601072
  – Calling Card (October 1976) Capo 108 ref. 7432 1601082
  – Photo Finish (1978) Capo 109 ref. 7432 1601092
  – Top Priority (September 1979) Capo 110 ref. 7432 1601102
  – Stage Struck (November 1980) Capo 111 ref. 7432 160112
  – Jinx (May 1982) Capo 112 ref. 7432 160122
  – Defender (1987) Capo 113 ref. 7432 160132
  – Fresh Evidence (1990) Capo 114 ref. 7432 160142

All these CDs have been remastered and have 2 bonus tracks
  – Edge in Blue (compilation) Capo ref. 7432 1627972
  – BBC Sessions Capo ref. 7432 1655492

Bootleg Series G-Men, Vol. 1:
  – Calling Card Part 1 (1992) G-MEN ESBCD 1B7/1
  – Calling Card Part 2 (1992) G-MEN ESBCD 1B7/2
  – The Bullfrog Interlude (1992) G-MEN ESBCD 1B7/3

Others
  – Off the Boards Capo/EPM/Le Castor Astral 984992
  – Taste (1969) Polydor 8411600-2
  – On the Boards (1970) Polydor 841599-2
  – Live Taste (1971) Polydor 841 602-2
  – Isle of Wight (1971) Polydor 841 601-2

Video – DVD Rory Gallagher Capo Video/distribution BMG
  – Irish Tour
  – Live in Cork

Rory Gallagher participated in the following recording sessions:
- BRING IT BACK HOME (1971) MIKE VERNON
- THE LONDON SESSIONS (1972) MUDDY WATERS
- THE SESSION, LONDON (1973) Vol. 1/2 JERRY LEE LEWIS
- LONDON REVISITED (1974) MUDDY WATERS & HOWLIN'WOLF
- LONDON REVISITED (1974) MUDDYWATERS
- LIVE (1975) ALBERT KING
- GAODHALS VISION (1977) JOEO'DONNELL
- PUTTING ON THE STYLE (1978) LONNIE DONNEGAN
- TAROT SUITE (1978) MIKE BATT
- BOX OF FROGS (1984) BOX OF FROGS
- STRANGE LAND (1986) BOX OF FROGS
- ECHOES IN THE NIGHT (1985) GARY BROOKER
- THE SCATTERING (1989) THE FUREYS & DAVEY ARTHUR
- OUTOFTHEAIR (1989) DAVYSPILLANE BAND
- WORDS AND MUSIC (1989) PHILCOUTER
- FLAGS AND EMBLEMS (1991) STIFF LITTLE FINGERS
- 30 YEARS A-GREYING (1992) THE DUBLINERS
- THE OUTSTANDING ALBUM (1993) THE CHRIS BARBER BAND
- STRANGERS ON THE RUN (1995) SAMUEL EDDY
- PAIN KILLER (1994) ENERGYORCHARD
- LEAVING TOWN BLUES/SHOWBIZ BLUES (1994) PETER GREEN SONGBOOK

Additional information on Rory Gallagher (equipment, concerts, biography, TV, fans, photos, links etc) can be found on the internet:
Main website: www.rorygallagher.com
www.btinternet.com/rory.gallagher
http://www.rory.de
http://www.top-priority.de

# Photographic Acknowledgements

REPORTERS ASSOCIES pages 112 a/b (collection JNC), 136 (collection JNC), 167a (collection JNC)

Jo CLAUWAERT pages 151, 156 a/b, 185

Jean-Noël COGHE pages 7, 36, 79, 89, 91, 92, 93, 95, 96, 97, 98, 107, 108, 109, 121, 122, 128, 131, 132 a/d, 142, 156c, 160, 161, 171, 173, 175, 178, 179a, 190, 192

Jean-Francois DISTASO pages 147, 180a

THE CORK EXAMINER page 10 (collection Donal Gallagher)

Donal GALLAGHER pages 144, 181

Frederic GUERRI page 163

Erik MACHIELSEN pages 57, 58, 60, 62, 66, 69, 71, 72, 132e

MANIA pages 182, 183, 184

Catherine MATTELAER pages 2, 56, 77, 100, 102, 112c, 118, 127, 129, 176, 177a/b, 180b/c, 191

MORRISS page 164c

STRANGE MUSIC pages 14, 18, 20, 24, 27, 28, 29, 30, 32, 35, 43, 115, 116, 137

Georges PIAT page 167b, document page 152, 164b

Jean-Louis RANCUREL pages 82, 90

DOCUMENTS JNC pages 44, 49, 50, 54, 55, 85, 94, 99, 104, 114, 162, 164a, 177c/d, 179b/c

# Other Books Consulted

*Les dieux du Blues*, Atlas publications

*Les Irlandais*, Sean O'Faolain, Coop Breizh (Penguin Books)

*Irlande, terre des Celtes*, Pierre Joannon, Ouest-France publications

*Contes et Légendes d'Irlande*, Georges Dottin, Terre de brumes

*Belfast Blues*, Richard Deutsch, Granit Noir, Terre de brumes

*La Clé de verre, La moisson rouge, Le faucon de Malte, L'Introuvable, Sang Maudit, Le grand braquage, Papier tue-mouches, Le sac de Gouffignal, Le dixième indice et autres enquetes du 'Continental Op'…* by Dashiell Hammett, Gallimard, collection Série Noire.

# THANKS

*(Disorder in order)*
Donal Gallagher, Cecilia Gallagher, Catherine Mattelaer, Roland Van Campenout, Gerry McAvoy, Tom O'Driscoll, Lou Martin, Rod de Ath, Brendan O'Neill, Ted McKenna, Tony Arnold, Mark Feltham, Jim Leverton, Wilgar Campbell, John Cooke, David Levy, Richard Newman …, and all the musicians who supported Rory.

Pascal Bernadin, Albert Warin, Jean Vanloo, I Cogoni, Le Plan, L'Aéronef, Marcq Culture, FNAC Nord-Est, L&S Muret and Co ..., Eric X and Stephan Bossa. Jean Yves Reuzeau, Raphael Caussimon, Marc Torralba, Yazid Manou, David Angevin and Benedicte Perot, Lorna Carson, Brian Steer, Anne Mortier, Marlon, Frederic Guerri, Philip Dhaussy, Mao-Salt-Tout, Tir Na Nog, and Debbie …

Erik Machielsen, Jean-Louis Rancurel, MANIA, Jean-Francois Distaso, Georges Piat, Jo Clauwaert and Lucie Dambrine.

*Rory and Roland*

*Rory in San Sebastian, May 1974*

*Rory Gallagher and Jean-Noël Coghe, Lille 1986*